The Negro Professional Class

BY

G. FRANKLIN EDWARDS

With a Foreword by OTIS DUDLEY DUNCAN

The Free Press of Glencoe, Illinois

FOREWORD

This monograph stands as a reminder that any effort to characterize the structure of a contemporary society in terms of its classes and ethnic groups yields at best a single "snapshot" of a historically moving process. At its worst, a structural analysis may convey a purely fictitious impression of stability and rigidity. The unfortunate tendency to divorce the studies of social organization and social change has been especially pronounced in recent research on social stratification. Where such research has dealt with mobility at all, mobility has often been conceived simply as the redistribution of personnel among disjunct layers of the social pyramid. As a methodological abstraction, this view of mobility has its uses. But to correct its partiality, there is a need for research on mobility as a process through which social structures are transformed.

Some understanding of the Negro professional group can be gained through a social trends analysis of already available data. Among the relevant trends which such data document are the growing importance of professional occupations in the total labor force of the national economy, the general movement toward proportional representation of the Negro in the professions as well as other occupations, the urbanization of the Negro, and the increasing educational opportunities and attainments of this minority group. At bottom, however, these social trends are but a summation of the converging movements of individuals. A full analysis of such a trend as the rise of a Negro middle class requires information on the origins, destinations, and intervening positions of those whose experiences add up to a modification of an earlier social structure. Thus Dr. Edwards' data shed light on a current of social change which has heretofore been widely recognized but seldom studied in sufficient detail.

One cannot refrain from commenting on the high quality of this research. It was the work of a single investigator, who was without extensive financial and organizational support. Yet rigorous--though simple--techniques of sampling, data collection, and analysis were employed. The result testifies to the important role of the lone research worker, who is being increasingly forgotten in this day of mass-produced "team" research. Working on a small scale, he can still make a significant contribution to the understanding of our society without resorting to haphazard observational techniques, impressionistic analysis, and merely speculative interpretations. It is a pleasure to be able to commend this study, on its scientific merits, to students of American society. Its social significance will be appreciated by those whose activities bring them into touch with the problematic aspects of the subject dealt with, but the author has wisely avoided confusing research with suggestions for social action.

Otis Dudley Duncan

The University of Chicago

AUTHOR'S PREFACE

As this monograph is a development of the author's doctoral
dissertation at the University of Chicago, its very nature places
him under a heavy obligation to many persons who contributed to
whatever of merit it possesses. Acknowledgment is made of the
helpful instruction received from faculty members of the Department of Sociology of the University of Chicago. I am particularly
indebted to the late Professor Louis Wirth, who served as chair-
man of the dissertation committee and who was the first to suggest
that the work warranted publication. Dr. Herbert Goldhamer, now
with the Rand Corporation, made many valuable suggestions during
the early stages of the work. Warm acknowledgment is made of
the assistance furnished by Drs. Otis Dudley Duncan and Albert J.
Reiss, Jr., who offered beneficial advice after reading the original
manuscript and who, otherwise, provided warm,friendly support
throughout the period of preparation. I am especially indebted to
Dr. Duncan for his consent to write the Foreword.

Through informal relations with my colleagues in the Department of Sociology at Howard University, I have received many
helpful suggestions. Special thanks are due Dr. Harry J. Walker
for his assistance during the period in which the project was set up
and for his continued interest in the work. My indebtedness to Dr.
E. Franklin Frazier goes beyond any identification which this work
has with his interests, though the kinship which the monograph
bears to Professor Frazier's writings will be recognized immediately. The opportunity for stimulating discussions with him has

6

done much to shape my own thinking on race relations and other subjects.

Mr. Jeremiah Kaplan of the Free Press has been a patient and understanding publisher. I am appreciative of his understanding attitude of the intervening factors which have served to delay the present publication.

Special thanks are due many other persons, too numerous to mention individually, for their contribution of technical services and other skills. I reserve a feeling of warm affection for the many respondents who took time from their busy programs to supply the data on which the monograph is based.

The development of a work of this type, limited as it is, imposes a heavy sacrifice upon those who live in closest association with the author. Perforce, such persons must share the author's anxieties and frustrations and live through them. I am grateful to my wife, Peggy, and to my daughter, Donalee Marie, who have borne with understanding the sacrifices they have been forced to make during the course of the preparation of this work.

It is hardly necessary to add that the author accepts full responsibility for the deficiencies of the work.

G. Franklin Edwards

Howard University

CONTENTS

Page

FOREWORD   3

AUTHOR'S PREFACE   5

LIST OF TABLES   11

CHAPTER

I. INTRODUCTION   17

    Occupational Orientation   21

    Emergence of Professional Functionaries . . .   23

    Summary   25

II. STATEMENT OF THE PROBLEM AND METHOD .   27

    Methods and Techniques   31

    Evaluation of Sample   40

    The Community   45

III. THE OVERALL PATTERN OF MOBILITY: OCCU-
PATIONAL ORIGINS AND INHERITANCE   49

    Comparisons with Other Studies of Mobility . .   56

    Generational Mobility   62

    Occupational Transmission   67

    Inheritance of Specific Occupations   67

    Transmission of Socio-Economic Status   70

8

Chapter		Page
IV.	FACTORS ASSOCIATED WITH MOBILITY	77
	Age as Related to Occupational Origin.	77
	Region of Origin	79
	The Influence of Father's Occupation	87
	Financial Status of Parents	94
	Financial Support of Education	94
	Educational Background of Respondents' Parents	101
	The Role of Color.	104
	Summary	113
V.	IMAGES AND MOTIVATIONS	117
	The Importance of the Social Structure	117
	Chief Motivation for Entering Field.	120
	Physicians and Dentists	122
	Lawyers.	133
	Teachers	138
	Summary	142
VI.	THE CAREER PROFILE	145
	Education	147
	Occupational Experiences	150
	Marriage and Family Characteristics	154
VII.	SUMMARY AND CONCLUSIONS	161
	Findings.	163
	Limitations and Overall Evaluation	170

Page

APPENDICES.   173

    A. Instrument Used in Study   175

    B. States Included in Each Region and Number of
        Respondents by States.   185

    C. Tables 37-50, Inclusive.   187

NOTES.   199

BIBLIOGRAPHY.   215

INDEX   221

LIST OF TABLES

Table   Page

1. Comparison of Respondents Living in Urban Places
   with the Total Negro Population (1910), by Size of
   Urban Community   43

2. Region of Origin of Sample Population and Total
   Negro Population, 1910   44

3. Regular Occupation of Respondents' Fathers, for all
   Respondents and for Each Professional Group, by
   Percent   50

4. Comparison of the Occupational Distribution of Re-
   spondents' Fathers with Occupational Distribution of
   Married Negro Male Workers 16 Years of Age and
   Over in 1910, Using the Method of Expected Cases   51

5. Comparison of the Occupational Distribution of Respondents' Fathers with the Occupational Distribution
   of Married Negro Male Workers (1910), Classified
   into White Collar, Blue Collar, and Farm Workers   53

6. Comparison of Occupational Distribution of Fathers
   of Respondents Born and Reared in the District of
   Columbia and Those Migrating There with All Married Negro Male Workers 16 Years of Age and Over
   for the District of Columbia in 1910   55

7. Comparison of the Occupational Distribution of the
   Fathers of Respondents from the District of Columbia
   with the Occupational Distribution of all Married Ne-
   gro Male Workers 16 Years of Age and Over in the
   District of Columbia for 1910, Classified into White
   Collar and Blue Collar Classes   56

8. Comparison of Occupational Origins of Respondents
   with the Occupational Origins of Professional Respondents in Two Other Studies of Mobility   57

12

Table   Page

9.   Occupational Origins of Respondents of Present
      Study Compared with the Occupational Origins of
      Professional Respondents in the National Opinion
      Research Center's Survey   61

10.   Occupational Distribution of Respondents' Paternal
      Grandfathers for the Entire Group and for Each
      Professional Group Shown Separately, by Percent   63

11.   Comparison of the Occupational Distribution of Re-
      spondents' Paternal Grandfathers with Those of
      Professional Respondents in the NORC Survey   66

12.   Transmission of Identical Occupations from Father
      to Son for All Professional Groups and for Each
      Group Shown Separately   69

13.   Respondents and Their Adult Siblings Having the
      Same Occupation as Their Fathers, for All Profes-
      sional Groups and for Each Group Shown Separately   69

14.   Occupational Distribution of Paternal Grandfathers,
      Fathers, and All Adult Sons, by Percent   71

15.   Percentage Distribution of the Occupations of Pa-
      ternal Grandfathers, Fathers, and All Adult Sons
      Classified into White Collar, Blue Collar, and
      Farm Groups, and Percentage Difference in These
      Groups from One Generation to Another   72

16.   Number and Percentage Distribution of Respondents
      Classified According to Age of Respondent and Oc-
      cupation of Father   78

17.   Occupational Origins of Respondents Classified
      According to Region of Origin, by Percent   80

18.   Occupational Distribution of All Adult Male Siblings
      According to Region of Origin, by Percent   85

19.   Occupational Distribution of All Adult Male Siblings
      According to Occupational Level of Father, by
      Percent   89

20.   Educational Attainment of Adult Male Siblings and
      Median School Years Completed by Siblings, Ac-
      cording to Occupational Level of Father   92

Table

21. Percentage Distribution of Parents of Respondents
     According to Income Class, for All Groups and for
     Each Professional Group Shown Separately   95

22. Chief Source of Income from Which Undergraduate
     Expenses Were Paid, According to Age Group   96

23. Contributions to the Undergraduate and Graduate
     Expenses of Respondents, According to Region and
     Source of Contribution, by Percent   98

24. Percentage of Adult Male Siblings Attaining Each
     Specified Level of Schooling and Median Years of
     Schooling Completed by Siblings, According to In-
     come Level of Father   100

25. Percentage Distribution of the Occupations of All
     Adult Male Siblings According to Income Level of
     Father, and Percentage Entering White Collar, Blue
     Collar, and Farm Occupations   101

26. Educational Attainment of Fathers According to Age
     of Respondent, by Percent   103

27. Percentage Distribution of Respondents According to
     Color, by Professional Group   109

28. Percentage Distribution of Respondents According to
     Color, Classified into Light, Brown, and Dark, by
     Professional Group   109

29. Percentage Distribution of Respondents According to
     Color, by Age Groups   112

30. Percentage Distribution of Respondents According to
     Color and Age (Regrouped)   112

31. Percentage Distribution of Respondents According to
     Chief Motivation for Entering Specified Profession,
     by Professional Group   121

32. Chief Source of Financial Assistance for Meeting Col-
     lege and Professional Expenses, According to Profes-
     sional Group, by Percent   128

33. Academic Rank of Physicians and Dentists in Their
     High School Classes   130

14

Table   Page

34.   Period in Which Decision to Enter Profession Was
      Made for Each of the Professional Groups, by Percent 131

35.   Level of First Job Following Collegiate Work, Ac-
      cording to Socio-Economic Level of Job and Profes-
      sional Group, by Percent   152

36.   Percentage Distribution of All Respondents According
      to Specified Number of Offspring, by Professional
      Group   156

37.   Percentage Distribution of Respondents According to
      Age and Professional Group   187

38.   Percentage of Fathers of Respondents Attaining Each
      Specified Level of Schooling and Median Years of
      Schooling for All Fathers According to Professional
      Group   188

39.   Percentage of Mothers of Respondents Attaining Each
      Specified Level of Schooling and Median Years of
      Schooling for All Mothers According to Professional
      Group   189

40.   Percentage of Spouses Attaining Each Specified Level
      of Schooling and Median Years of Schooling Completed
      by Spouses, for All Spouses According to Professional
      Group   190

41.   Percentage Distribution of Respondents Classified
      According to Sources from Which Financial Assistance
      for Meeting College and Professional Expenses Were
      Obtained   191

42.   Percentage Distribution of Respondents According to
      Age at Which Bachelor's Degree Was Received and
      Median Age at Time of Receiving Degree, by Profes-
      sional Group   193

43.   Percentage Distribution of Those Not Completing the
      Bachelor's Degree According to Age at Which Pre-
      Professional Training Was Completed and Median Age
      at Time of Completion, by Professional Group   193

44.   Percentage Distribution of Respondents According to
      Age at Which Professional Degree Was Received, and
      Average Age at Which Degree Was Completed, by
      Professional Group   194

Table

45. Percentage Distribution of Respondents According to
    Age at Which Work in Present Professional Field Was
    Begun and Average Age of Beginning, by Professional
    Group   194

46. Number of Years Intervening between High School and
    College and Mean Number of Years Out-of-School for
    the Entire Group of Respondents and for Those with
    Interrupted Experiences, by Professional Group   195

47. Number of Years Intervening between Completion of
    Pre-Professional Work and Beginning of Professional
    Training, and Average Number of Years Out-of-School
    for All Respondents and for Those with Interrupted
    Experiences, by Professional Group   196

48. Percentage Distribution of Respondents According to
    Age at Time of (First) Marriage and Average Age at
    Time of Marriage, by Professional Group   197

49. Percentage Distribution of Respondents According to
    Age at Birth of First Child and Average Age at Time of
    Birth, by Professional Group   197

50. Percentage Distribution of Respondents According to
    Marital Status, by Professional Group   198

I.

INTRODUCTION

This monograph is a study of occupational mobility among
Negroes in a selected group of professional occupations in the District of Columbia. It is designed along the lines of traditional
studies in the field of occupational mobility and seeks to provide
information and knowledge on the social origins of persons entering professional occupations, certain social characteristics of the
group, the amount of mobility demonstrated by them as measured
by the difference between their occupational level and those of
their fathers and grandfathers, and on the career pattern which is
typical for members of the group. Some attention is given, also,
to an analysis of the motivations and incentives which operated to
define the occupational aspirations of the group and have led to the
selection of careers in the professional fields studied.

It should be indicated at the outset that in selecting the professions as a particular class of occupations for study, no attempt
is made to evaluate the total occupational structure of Negroes;
nor is it the purpose of this study to assess the total amount of
mobility occurring within that structure. The selection of the professions for study has been dictated in large part by the attempt to
relate our findings on occupational mobility to some of the current
theories of social stratification and mobility. Functionaries in the
professional fields selected for study are taken as representatives
of the Negro middle class. [1] It is thought that from a knowledge of
the factors associated with the selection and recruitment of Negroes for work in professional occupations, some insight is

provided into the process by which the Negro group has developed a differentiated middle class based upon occupational status and its correlates of income and education. Since one central idea of this work is the association of professional functionaries with a given status group in the Negro community, it becomes necessary to establish the basis of this identification before turning to the major problems and methods employed in this study.

The social structure of Negro life has always shown some social differentiation, if not marked stratification. There existed among the slaves social distinctions based upon the type of work performed and the degree of skill necessary for such work. House servants and artisans, for example, enjoyed somewhat greater prestige and privileges than did the mass of field slaves. [2] There was, moreover, a sharp distinction between the slaves and free persons, the latter group numbering approximately a half million persons at the time of the Emancipation. [3] In addition to the functional and legal bases of differentiation, skin color was also a factor in the distinctions which were drawn among elements of the Negro population. A high valuation was placed upon a light complexion. On the whole, house servants were lighter in color than field hands, and free persons were lighter than slaves. [4] Early gradations on the whole were based primarily on "status" distinctions and not upon clearly delineated socio-economic values.

The above remarks are not intended to imply that property distinctions were not present among Negroes. Free Negroes had entered numerous business undertakings prior to the Emancipation and, according to Harris' account, [5] had accumulated, in some instances, what amounted to small fortunes. As landowners and farmers, caterers, building contractors, liverymen, tailors,

barbers, and inn keepers, they demonstrated an interest in business ventures, and there developed among them an ideology which
regarded business enterprise as an avenue to economic independence. This interest in business persisted after the Emancipation,
when Negro banks and business associations developed.

Despite the initial enthusiasm and optimism regarding the
possibilities of capital accumulation through business enterprise,
a substantial business community among this minority did not develop. This failure, Harris states,[6] was owing mainly to the kinds
of establishments operated by Negroes. If banks and insurance
companies are excluded, Negro business enterprises fall mainly
into four categories: amusement and recreational enterprises,
real estate, retail trade, and personal service. These are poor
credit risks. In this connection, Frazier adds that one of the underlying reasons for the failure of Negro business to develop on a significant scale is the lack of an entrepreneurial tradition among
members of the group.[7] Other writers on the subject have called
attention to the factors cited above as important in the failure of
Negroes to develop large-scale business enterprises.[8]

Whatever be the underlying reasons for the failure of a significant proprietor class to develop among this group, the fact remains, as Myrdal pointed out, that while both business enterprises
and the professions have developed mainly as monopolies under
segregation, generally the Negro community has supported a larger number of professional functionaries than business entrepre-
neurs or proprietors.[9]

The failure to develop a substantial economic base for a
middle class left the professional occupations as the chief group of
occupations in the Negro community which could be identified with

the American middle class. Frazier observes that the Negro class structure has become more highly differentiated in the Northern and Border cities than in Southern cities, and that as occupational status has come to replace "social" status factors as a basis of class identification, the Negro "middle" class is composed of professional persons, business men, and those engaged in clerical occupations. He adds, "However, in viewing the growth of the middle class, it should be pointed out that its growth has been greatest in the professions and in clerical services and least in trade or business enterprise, which has generally been the basis of its power."[10] In this respect, the Negro middle class has a somewhat different historical background from the middle classes of other groups in Western society.[11]

It would be a relatively easy task--but one hardly considered important here--to assemble a mass of factual data in support of the proposition that a differentiated middle class based upon socio-economic values among Negroes should properly consider persons in the professions, rather than those identified with business or clerical work, if only one occupational category is considered. Suffice it to point out that in terms of the number of Negroes employed in these respective occupational categories in 1950, professional and kindred workers numbered 179,198; those in business, 94,966; and the clerical and sales group, 250,606.[12] The numbers employed in these categories represented 3.3, 1.8, and 4.7 percent, respectively, of a total of 5,376,917 employed Negro workers in 1950. It should be noted that in 1950 the number of Negro workers in clerical and sales functions exceeded the number in professional occupations for the first time, a fact owing to the great expansion of clerical occupations during the War period and to the increased demand for workers in this area in a period of acute labor shortage. In 1940, for example, the number of Negroes classed as professional workers exceeded the number classified in clerical positions by approximately 17,000. [13]

If the number of Negroes in these respective occupational categories is related to all employed workers represented by these categories, and not alone to the occupational statistics of Negroes, the relative importance of the professional group in the occupations identified with the middle class becomes more apparent. Thus, in 1950, Negro professional workers represented 3.8 percent of all such workers. Negro clerical and sales workers represented 2.3 percent of all workers in that category. Only 1.8 percent of all workers classed as proprietors were Negroes. [14]

The above figures are meaningful inasmuch as we are considering the origin of class in a socio-economic sense rather than an emergent based upon social status considerations only. The percentages cited above indicate that it is in the professional category that the Negro group has made the greatest dent in the middle class occupational structure. It should be added that among Negroes professionals are accorded greater community prestige than are proprietors and clerical workers, a fact which is suggested by the vocational aspirations of Negro students. The preferences registered by them are obviously related to their views of the social structure of Negro life and reflect in part their evaluation of the prestige to be gained from following the occupations selected.

Occupational Orientation

The studies of vocational choices of Negro youth indicate that they are oriented mainly toward professional occupations. Doubtless

the most significant data on this subject are the findings of the
United States Office of Education's study of higher education among
Negroes. [15]   The study revealed that 81 percent of a total of 2,942
freshmen and approximately 82 percent of 1,001 seniors in Negro
colleges registered as their choices occupations classed as professional or semi-professional. Business and clerical occupations
were the selections of 7.6 percent of the freshmen and 11.5 percent
of the seniors. Less than one percent of the freshmen and 1.7 percent of the seniors desired to enter the public service. While 9.6
percent of the freshmen elected one of the trades or mechanic arts
as a preferred choice, only 2.6 percent of the seniors picked an
occupation in this category. It is significant that only 1.8 and 2.3
percent of the freshmen and seniors, respectively, selected farming and allied occupations as their primary choice. [16]

These findings are similar to those of other studies of the
vocational aspirations of Negro youth. Johnson, for example, indicated that 61.8 percent of Negro high school students in various
parts of the country selected a professional occupation as the field
they would like to enter. [17]   The same orientation is held by Negro
rural youth in the South, as revealed in a study made by the same
author. Thirty-eight percent of the male youth and 65 percent of
the female youth studied by the author in rural areas of that region
desired to enter a professional field, although, significantly, only
about two-thirds of the males and approximately the same proportion
of the females making such a choice expected eventually to engage
in work on this level.

The preponderant choice of professional occupations registered
by Negro youth is, to a large extent, similar to the choices of other
groups in the society, particularly those of second-generation

immigrants. From the time of the pioneering study of Counts in
1925 to the present, the occupational orientation of high school and
college students has been toward the professions. [18]

Despite the tendency for the choices made by Negroes to resemble those of other groups, some variations respecting the occupational choices of Negro and other youth should be pointed out.
There are, for example, certain occupations listed in the recent
survey by the National Opinion Research Center [19] as enjoying the
highest prestige values which are seldom mentioned by Negroes.
Reference is made here to some of the highest positions in national,
state, and local governments--Supreme Court Justice, cabinet of-
ficer, diplomat, positions in the foreign service, Congressman,
and mayor of a large city. These positions as a group enjoy
slightly higher prestige, as evaluated by a nationwide cross-section
of the population, than did a wide range of professional occupations.
This means, simply, that the occupational orientation of Negroes,
to a greater extent than characterizes other groups in the population, is focused more sharply on the professions than on other high
prestige occupations as an attempt is made to move upward in the
social system.

The Emergence of Professional Functionaries

Professional functionaries among Negroes began to appear in
substantial numbers after the Civil War. Their appearance was
dependent upon the presence of a permissive educational climate
and the development of Negro institutions of higher learning, which
evolved chiefly from missionary and philanthropic efforts during
the Reconstruction period. Though both Johnson and Woodson note
that some professional functionaries appeared in the pre-Civil War

period, the number was very small and limited mainly to the free Negro population.[20] Whereas free Negroes could enter some fields with a minimum of training, qualification for work in a professional field demanded somewhat more formal schooling. Education for Negroes was viewed with disfavor by those in control of the social system. Indeed, public education at the higher levels, even in the North, was not so popular and widespread as today.

The development of a professional group among Negroes is best indicated by the statistics on the number of college and professional graduates. By 1876, there were only 314 such graduates, with 96 of this number holding professional degrees. The increase since that date has been continuous, but Negro college and professional graduates did not number a thousand annually until the second decade of the present century.[21]

Clergymen and teachers appeared as early as 1866, and these two professions claimed most of the graduates of the period 1868 to 1880. Physicians and dentists began to appear as early as 1870, but their numbers remained small for some time thereafter. Between 1890 and 1900 the number of Negro physicians doubled, from 909 to 1,734,[22] and was nearly doubled again in the following decade, when the total reached 3,409.[23] In the four decades since 1910, the increase in the number of Negro physicians has been relatively small, with the 1950 census reporting a total of 4,026.[24] Though some few lawyers were found during the Reconstruction period, the number of Negroes identified with the legal profession has remained rather small; only 1,450 were enumerated at the time of the last census.[25] Social workers began to appear around the turn of the century, and the number of such workers has increased rapidly since that time.[26] In other professional fields, there has been a rather slow development. In general, Negroes in professional occupations have been concentrated in the old line professions --medicine, teaching, the clergy. It is only at the present time, for example, that larger numbers are entering physical science research and the engineering professions.

In reviewing the growth of the professions among Negroes, Reid, summarizing the statistics for the half century since 1900, estimates that the number of professional workers increased by 161 percent, while the Negro population increase for the same period was 52 percent.[27] During the period under consideration, the number of dentists increased 750 percent; teachers, 229 percent; physicians and surgeons, 130 percent; lawyers, 65 percent; and clergymen, 12 percent.[28]

Professional workers among Negroes have not been uniformly distributed among the various sections of the country. The South has the largest proportion of teachers and clergymen, owing mainly to the traditionally segregated patterns of educational and religious life in the area. The South has, however, less than its proportionate share of physicians, dentists, social workers, and lawyers.[29] The migration of Negroes to the cities of the North and Border states during and following the first World War led to the formation of large Negro communities in these areas, increased the prospects for employment in industry, and created the economic base for the support of a substantial corps of professional functionaries.[30]

Summary

The chief concern of this brief introduction has been to point out that there are good reasons for studying Negroes in the professions if we are to get an accurate picture of the process by which this group has developed a differentiated middle class. It has been noted that (1) a middle class based upon business failed to develop on a significant scale among this minority; (2) the Negro professional group, though today not numerically larger than the clerical group, furnishes most of its leaders and is the single most important group among the white collar occupational categories when we consider the proportion that Negroes in one of these categories represent of all workers in the category; and (3) Negroes, like most native Americans and second-generation immigrants, are focused on professional fields as vocational choices, but Negroes hold the professions in somewhat sharper focus because of conditions peculiar to Negro life.

The chapter which follows provides a statement of the problem analyzed and furnishes an exposition of the methods employed. Succeeding chapters consider "The Overall Pattern of Mobility: Occupational Origins and Inheritance," "Factors Associated with Mobility," "Images and Motivations," and "The Career Profile." These are followed by a brief chapter which summarizes the findings.

II.

STATEMENT OF THE PROBLEM AND METHOD

It has been previously observed that the Negro group began
the period of freedom with a rather amorphous social structure, and
that functionaries to meet the needs of a segregated community life
had to be developed rather rapidly as a consequence. This development has occurred within the relatively short period of three generations, if a generation be considered as approximately 30 years.
It is suggested that the exigencies of this situation demanded a considerable amount of vertical social mobility if the service needs of
the group were to be met. The amount of social mobility occurring
within such a nascent social structure becomes one of the central
problems of this study. Stated otherwise, we are concerned with
the amount of mobility which occurs in a social system which is
highly undifferentiated at the outset, but which has a need of supply-
ing professional services rather rapidly as community life develops.

The literature of social mobility suggests that in a fluid social
system, such as that represented by Negro life, vertical mobility
is somewhat greater than in more stable and crystallized systems.
A comparative study of the achievement of eminence in England and
in the United States discovered that a larger percentage of persons
of low status origins were able to enter eminence fields in the latter
country, owing to the greater degree of fluidity present. [1] The findings of the studies of mobility patterns among second-generation
immigrants, who show a greater degree of occupational mobility
than native Americans, also support the proposition mentioned above.[2]

- 27 -

It should be expected, then, that the observed mobility pattern for the group under study will deviate from that found for native whites and will resemble more the pattern which has been observed for other minorities.

Inasmuch as increased differentiation and a greater degree of stratification are the result of certain dynamic factors at work, both within a group and in the relationship of the group to the total society, a comparison of the status origins of the subjects with those of their fathers and grandfathers should provide information on the manner in which mobility patterns change with time and thus furnish insight into the process by which status groups are formed. In this connection, a comparison of the status origins of the older and younger subjects also should furnish useful information on the process. It is expected that the younger subjects will have a smaller percentage of persons of low status origins than would be the case of the older ones. Such evidence, if established, suggests that over a period of time any group is likely to develop a more crystallized stratification pattern. This fact accounts very largely, we believe, for the differences in observed social mobility between second-generation immigrants and native Americans.

This aspect of the problem may now be stated in the form of the following questions: in the development of a professional structure, does the social system of Negro life recruit persons of lower socio-economic origin as a result of peculiar historical forces connected with the experiences of the group than is the case among native whites and other groups in the population? Is it possible to discern the manner in which a social system, largely undifferentiated at the outset, evolves a crystallized stratification pattern?

In comparing the subjects of the present study with professional persons of other groups, it should be expected that marked
similarities will be observed owing to the homogeneous character
of the occupations considered. But even within this limited range
of occupations, some variations may be expected in the comparisons.
Hatt[3] raised the general question of the nature of the stratification
system of the mass society and concerned himself with possible fruit-
ful approaches for more definitive answers than we now possess regarding the phenomenon. His formulation took account of the varying
dimensions--power, economics, status--which must be considered
in approaching the problem of stratification in complex societies.
Central to Hatt's conceptualization is the idea that the stratification
pattern of any local community will show strong resemblances to
the prevailing pattern of the total society, but owing to the differences in the importance attached to the stratification variables by
different communities, some variation from the dominant pattern
may be observed.

The same question was raised, at approximately the same
time, by Florence Kluckhohn[4] in her consideration of dominant and
substitute profiles of cultural orientations, as gained from the following paragraph:

> ...In every American community, no matter how large or how
> well within the main current of economic or other creative ac-
> tivity it may be, there are segments of the population which
> live in partial accordance with other orientations than those
> which constitute the dominant profile. Even the largest and
> most rapidly developing communities have their upper class,
> or classes. We must know more than we now do about the num-
> ber of such groups and most especially must seek to discover
> the way in which their structuring is related, first to that of
> the total community, and then to the system as a whole.[5]

Duncan and Artis,[6] after an analysis of the stratification pattern of
a local community in Pennsylvania, consider the general question of
the relationship between the observed pattern for the local community and that described for the larger society and reach the following
conclusion:

> The social structure of the mass society implies a pattern of
> stratification based on socioeconomic and political power and
> a system of invidious prestige values which are roughly uni-
> form throughout the society. Insofar as regions and localities
> are economically, ecologically, and politically specialized,
> variations in the general pattern of stratification will appear;
> but they are to be understood precisely as variants of the gen-
> eral pattern.[7]

It is our belief that what applies to regions and localities applies as well to ethnic groups which, in Kluckhohn's terms, are likely
to "live in partial accordance with other orientations than those
which constitute the dominant profile." As mentioned above, the
mobility pattern for the Negro minority should be influenced by
forces operating in the total society and, to this extent, the pattern
should show features which resemble that discovered for other
groups. But owing to certain peculiar historical experiences of the
group and to its status in the society, some variations should be expected.

It is necessary to add that this study uses many of the variables commonly employed in studies of occupational mobility: viz.,
age of respondent, occupational level of father, income of family,
and region of origin. But we shall be concerned with one variable
not considered by other studies. In the present investigation, attention must be given to skin color as a factor influencing mobility, as
this factor has exercised some influence in Negro life. The literature suggests that for a considerable period following their Emancipation, mulattoes, or persons of light color, held a disproportionate

share of the high prestige jobs in the Negro community. This resulted largely from certain social and economic advantages which
this group enjoyed prior to the Emancipation which gave them a
headstart during the period of freedom. There is the suggestion,
also, that with the urbanization of the Negro population less attention is given to skin color, so that the early advantages enjoyed by
the mulattoes have been lost, and a larger proportion of persons of
darker color have entered high level jobs in the last generation.
Our data permit us to test this hypothesis.

Methods and Techniques

To test the amount and direction of mobility within the Negro
group as a professional structure evolved, the first consideration
was to select a representative group of professional occupations and
of persons within those occupations for study. Certain qualifying
conditions were apparent at the outset. It was necessary to select,
first, a group of occupations in which males were highly represented.
This condition was necessary if comparisons with other studies
were to be made. Virtually every study in the field has considered
only the male population, with occupational transmission considered through the male line only. The logic of this selection is clear.
Women have only recently entered the labor force in significant
numbers. For a long period of our history the role definition for
this sex made a career subordinate to marriage and domestic duties.
It was necessary to eliminate social work from consideration, for
most workers identified with this profession are females.

Another limiting condition was that the training requirements
for performance in the profession be fairly uniform and of a high
order. To meet this condition, the clergy was eliminated. Although

there are many well-trained ministers in the community, a great many others have little or no professional training and, in some instances, little formal education. This latter conditions holds especially for ministers serving the sectarian churches or cults. In this connection--the employment of high level training as a criterion--it was decided to select college teachers rather than teachers in the elementary and secondary schools as representatives of the teaching profession.

A final criterion was that a sufficiently large number of males be present in the profession to allow for the selection of a group large enough to make possible the study of the relationship of certain variables to mobility through statistical breakdowns or subclassification. This criterion eliminated a number of professional occupations from consideration.[8] The labor force statistics for 1940 show that there were only four actors, fourteen architects, twelve engineers, eleven chemists, and similar small numbers in other professional occupations.[9] These numbers were too small to allow for cross-tabulations in those instances where we wished to study variations between or among the professional fields themselves.

The occupations which qualified for this study from the viewpoint of numbers, as enumerated by the census, were (1) clergymen, (2) college presidents, professors, and instructors, (3) physicians and surgeons, (4) dentists, (5) lawyers and judges, (6) teachers, musicians, and music teachers. With the exception of the clergy, eliminated for the reason furnished above, these professions were selected for study. As mentioned previously, college teachers were used to represent the teacher group. The professional occupations in which Negroes are most highly represented in the District of

Columbia are those in which the group has the largest numerical
representation in the labor force statistics for the country as a
whole. [10]

Having determined the professional occupations to be studied,
it was then necessary to select a representative group of persons
at work in these occupations from whom desired information could
be obtained. The Sixteenth Census labor force statistics for the
District of Columbia gave the following totals for Negroes in the
occupations selected: college presidents, professors, and instructors, 107; physicians and surgeons, 187; dentists, 64; and lawyers
and judges, 73. The prospect that a considerable change had occurred in the number of persons in each of these occupations since
the 1940 census was taken demanded that some means be devised
for securing a more accurate count of the population in these respective occupations. Since the physicians, dentists, and lawyers
each have professional associations, a first step was to secure
membership lists from these organizations. The rosters of the
associations showed a larger number in each of the categories than
was enumerated by the Sixteenth Census. It was apparent from inspection that a portion of the difference between the figures of the
Sixteenth Census and those furnished by the associations' rosters
was owing to the latter's inclusion of persons of both sexes and
individuals living outside the District of Columbia, chiefly in
neighboring communities in Maryland and Virginia. The membership lists of the respective professional associations gave the following totals: physicians, 211; dentists,92; and lawyers, 181. The
lists were studied with the secretaries or other responsible officers
of the organizations and the following classes eliminated: women,
those not living or practicing in the District of Columbia, those

who had moved to other communities, and those who had died since
the roster was drawn up for the year.

The compilation of a list of lawyers from which a sample might
be drawn represented something of a special problem. Of the 181
persons listed as members of the Washington Bar Association, not
all of them were persons actively engaged in the practice of law, or
even in work which was primarily of a legal nature. Many of these
persons were engaged in real estate or some other type of business,
while others were employed by the Federal Government. Still others worked in one capacity or another and practiced law at odd hours,
usually during the evening. (This latter category is referred to by
those in the profession as "Sundowners.") Our objective was to secure, as nearly as possible, an accurate list of persons with legal
training actively engaged in the practice of the law. For this reason a number of persons were eliminated from the Bar Association's
roster, although many of the "Sundowners" remained on the list. It
was recognized that many of the "Sundowners" were young lawyers
who were just beginning in the profession and whose practices were
not yet sufficiently remunerative to permit their leaving other employment which furnished a substantial portion of their income.

A search was then begun for persons engaged in the above
professions, but who were not members of the respective associations. It was discovered that most of the professional functionaries
were nominally identified with their respective professional bodies,
so that it was necessary to make only a few additions, less than ten
for each of the groups for which we had membership lists. After
eliminations and additions, the following totals were used: physicians, 190; dentists, 92 (eliminations and additions being equal);
and lawyers, 144.

The teachers who qualify for the study are connected with Howard University and Miner Teachers College, the latter a four-year college engaged very largely in the preparation of teachers for the District of Columbia. Only male teachers in the College of Liberal Arts and the Graduate School at Howard University were selected, inasmuch as the teacher qualifications in the other schools--engineering, music, religion, etc.--varied widely from those for teachers in the arts and sciences. Lists of teachers in the two institutions were assembled, and all male teachers included for study. All but eight of the teachers were members of the Howard faculty. Our total of 92 for this group is smaller than the 107 reported by the Sixteenth Census. While the difference may be accounted for by an actual reduction in the number of male teachers since the time of the Census' enumeration, it is more likely that the variation results from the Census' inclusion of male college teachers other than those in the arts and sciences.

From the assembled lists it was a relatively easy job to select a random sample of respondents for each professional group. Random numbers were drawn[11] with a few more numbers drawn than respondents desired, thus allowing for refusals.

The sample as selected includes 300 professional respondents, divided among the professions studied as follows: 90 physicians, 46 dentists, 72 lawyers, and 92 college teachers. The sample proportions represent 47 percent of the estimated universe of physicians, 50 percent of the dentists, and 50 percent of the lawyers. All of the known male college teachers of arts and science subjects are included in the study. It will be recognized that inasmuch as all teachers are included and only approximately one-half of the members of each of the other professional groups, the sample, as it stands, would yield

a somewhat inaccurate picture of the factors studied for the total
group of respondents owing to the disproportionate contribution of
the teachers. Adjustments have been made, therefore, in those instances where for the factors studied teachers have been found to
differ significantly from the other groups. These corrections have
involved the preparation of estimates by inflating the sizes of the
other groups to their universe proportions, and in all such instances
the results have been reported as estimates. Owing to the rather
homogeneous character of the occupations studied, the variations
between the prepared estimates and the results of the sample as
drawn, without correction, are exceedingly small. It must be emphasized that wherever comparisons are made between occupations,
estimates are not necessary, so that they have been prepared only
for the totals in those cases where teachers differ significantly
from the rest of the sample.

The data of the study were gathered by use of a schedule and
through interviews. The subjects selected on the basis of random
numbers were called by telephone and appointments made. Usually,
the interview occurred at the respondent's office, but most interviews took place either before the beginning of regular hours or at
the close of the office hour. Teachers were seen in their offices at
the institution where they were employed. There were few excep-
tions to this general procedure. Occasionally a respondent was
interviewed at home, but not more than a half dozen such interviews
were conducted, so that the interview situation is not believed to
have a significant influence on the materials gathered. Each respondent was seen for an average of approximately forty minutes, at
which time the schedule was completed and the interview conducted.
Since the schedule could be completed rather quickly, most of the

time was given over to asking a series of structured questions per-
taining to incentives, motivations, family life, schooling of the respondent, and to the careers of their siblings. The schedule was
completed and the interview conducted, always, at the same appointment.

The data were gathered in the period between June and Octo-
ber, 1950. Most of the field work had been completed by September, 1950; but the absence from the community of a number of
persons included in the sample necessitated the interviewing of
those few cases upon their return.

The schedule employed in the study appears as Appendix "A".
It was originally intended that the instrument would be used as a
mailed questionnaire, but later the decision was made to have the
investigator administer it. One finds, therefore, certain explana-
tory materials on the instrument which were designed to make clear
to the respondent the nature of the study had the instrument been
used as a questionnaire. Pre-tests were made on a small sample
of persons in late May and early June. A study of the pre-test
results suggested the wisdom of modifying a few of the original
items. By and large, changes were few and concerned the form
more than the content of the questions. The most significant change
was the addition of a series of questions requesting information on
the respondent's spouse. The dependence on other studies of mobility and related subjects for the form of many of the questions appear-
ing in the instrument will be apparent to those familiar with the literature.

A code for classifying the occupations used in this study was
developed from the code of occupational titles used in connection
with the labor force statistics of the Sixteenth Census, and the

occupational classes of that census employed rather than the Edwards classification of gainful workers into socio-economic groups. [12] The latter classification has been used in most studies of occupational mobility. The decision to use the occupational classification of the Sixteenth Census was made after it was discovered that conversion from this classification to the Edwards grouping could be made for comparing our results with those of other studies without serious difficulty and without measurable loss of accuracy. [13] One major advantage of using the occupational classes of the Sixteenth Census is that it discriminates more sharply than does the Edwards classification among the semiskilled and unskilled occupations. In setting up the study we were desirous of having a classification which would reveal, somewhat easily, various levels on which the fathers of the respondents worked other than the mere knowledge that they were semiskilled or unskilled workers. Another advantage of the classification used is that it separates the farmers, owners and tenants, from the proprietor group. Under the Edwards grouping farm owners and tenants are grouped with proprietors. Although many of our comparisons make use of the general classes of "white collar" and "blue collar" workers, the employment of the detailed classification of the Sixteenth Census served a useful purpose during the early phases of the study by providing insights into the specific areas within the unskilled and semiskilled categories where the fathers and siblings of the respondents are found.

The occupation of the fathers of the respondents was recorded for two periods, when the father was thirty years of age and again when he was fifty. The chief point of taking the occupation at two different time periods was to discern whether the father's occupation had shifted between the two ages. It was assumed that by age thirty most fathers had just started in an occupation, but that the occupation recorded for age fifty was likely to represent his regular or usual occupation. In those few instances where the father died before reaching the age of fifty, the occupation reported for the earlier period was used. Few men are out of the labor force at fifty; consequently, except for deaths and a few cases of disability, most of the fathers' occupations are those reported when the father was fifty years of age.

Our classification of region of origin of the respondents into South, North, and Border does not correspond to the regional classification used by the Bureau of the Census. The South, as used in this study, includes all of the states included in the Census' classification of South Atlantic, East South Central, and West South Central, except Delaware, Maryland, and the District of Columbia which are included in our Border group. Other states included in our Border group are Indiana, Missouri, West Virginia, and Kansas. All other states are classified into North and West, there being few respondents who were born in the West. The logic underlying the placement of the states of the Upper South in the Border group is that in these areas--in Maryland, Delaware, and the District of Columbia, chiefly--the Negro has had a somewhat different community experience, especially with regard to education, than that experienced in the other Southern states.[14] The states included in each region are enumerated in Appendix "B".

Color is rated on a six point scale ranging from very light to very dark. Attention was given to the work of Parrish[15] in developing the scale, and his original seven-point scale was reduced to six points. Our objective was not to record the color of the person in such rigorous terms as the study done by Parrish with the scale demanded. We were concerned, rather, with getting a sufficiently accurate place on a continuum, ranging from very light to very dark, at which the respondent placed. Our original color evaluations were reclassified into groupings which involved the combination of several color classes, a fact which is given attention at the point in the text where this variable is discussed. As all color ratings were done by the investigator, biases occurring with respect to them are systematic ones. The reduction of the original six-point scale to three points through regrouping provided a further safeguard against possible errors of perception and/or judgment in the ratings.

The statistical techniques used in the study involve mainly measures of central tendencies and methods for testing the significance of observed differences. Wherever the significance of observed differences is tested, chi-square or the critical ratio is used, depending upon the demands of the data. Values qualifying at the five percent probability level are accepted as significant. In comparing the occupational level of the fathers of the respondents with the married Negro males in the labor force at the time at which the subjects were born, the method of expected cases is used to develop an index for the comparison.

Evaluation of the Sample

The representativeness of the sample must rest with the manner in which it was drawn. There are no known studies of the universe from which the sample was drawn with which its characteristics may be compared. Despite this, some of the characteristics of the sample should be pointed out.

The mean age of the group studied is approximately forty-six years (45. 6). The range in mean ages is from 43. 9 years for

teachers to 47.3 for physicians. The mean ages for dentists and
lawyers are 46.7 and 44.9 years, respectively. The mean ages for
physicians and lawyers may be compared with those reported by
Hartshorn[16] for a larger group of Negro physicians (182) and lawyers (221) for the country as a whole. The mean ages for physicians
and lawyers in the Hartshorn study were 49.2 and 46.7 years, respectively. The respondents of the present study are, therefore,
somewhat younger than those studied by Hartshorn, the difference
in mean ages being approximately two years for each of the two
groups. Though this difference appears small, it would be desirable to test for significance, a fact which is not possible owing to
Hartshorn's failure to report his sigma values. It should be observed that the lawyers are approximately two years younger than
the physicians for both Hartshorn's sample and for the present one.

The mean number of years of formal schooling for our sample was 19.2 years. The range was from 19.3 for physicians to
18.3 for dentists and lawyers, a difference of one year. The
mean number of years of schooling for teachers was 19.1 years.
Again, it is possible to compare our means for physicians and lawyers with those reported for these groups in the Hartshorn study.
The physicians studied by Hartshorn averaged 18.6 years of schooling; the lawyers had an average of 17.3 years of formal education.
Our subjects in these two groups have more formal training, on
the average seven-tenths of one year in the case of physicians and
one year in the case of the lawyers. The difference between the
average amount of formal education of physicians and lawyers in
the Hartshorn group was 1.3 years as compared with a difference
of one year for the two groups in the present study. Of particular
significance is the fact that the direction of the difference is the

same for both samples, with physicians having more formal education than lawyers.

As regards a number of other factors, our sample shows the characteristics of professional populations in general, e. g. , marital status, age at first marriage, and number of children. [17] Approximately ninety percent (89. 9) of our subjects were married, five percent (4. 72) were single, two percent (1. 77) widowed, three percent (3. 12) divorced, and four-tenths of one percent (0. 4) separated. The mean age at first marriage was 27. 5 years, while the mean number of children was 1. 19 for those who were ever married and 1. 13 for the entire group.

Inasmuch as at a later point we compare the population studied with the total Negro population in accounting for certain features which make the former a distinctive group in terms of achievement, it is well to observe at this point one characteristic which sharply distinguishes the sample from the rest of the Negro population. In comparing the areal distribution of the sample with that of the total Negro population at the mean year of birth of the former, it is discovered that the respondents of the study are more highly urban in origin. (The distribution of the Negro population in 1910 is used for the comparison. The mean age of 45. 6 years of the subjects places their mean year of birth almost midway between the 1900 and 1910 censuses. By using data from the 1910 Census we overestimate the urban character of the total Negro population, as it was more urbanized in 1910 than in 1900. The difference between the sample and total population with regard to the degree of urbanization is, therefore, underestimated.)

Approximately three-quarters of the subjects of this study (75. 7 percent) were born in communities of more than 2,500 persons,

while the remaining 24. 3 percent were born in rural areas. The
distribution of the Negro population in 1910 was almost the reverse
of this pattern; 72. 6 percent of all Negroes at that time lived in rural
communities, and 27. 4 percent were urban dwellers. Moreover, the
sample population came from urban communities of larger sizes than
characterized the distribution of the Negro population as shown below.

Table 1

Comparison of Respondents Living in Urban Places
with the Total Negro Urban Population (1910),
according to Size of Urban Community

| Size of Community | Percentage Distribution of Urban Population | | |
	Sample Population	Negro Population (1910)*	Difference
2, 500 - 9, 999	11. 3	6. 7	4. 6
10, 000 - 24, 999	10. 7	4. 2	6. 5
25, 000 - 99, 999	14. 0	6. 1	7. 9
100, 000 - 499, 999	31. 0	6. 4	24. 6
500, 000 and over	8. 7	4. 0	4. 7
Total	75. 7	27. 4	48. 3

* Source: Bureau of the Census, Negro Population in the United
States, 1790-1915 (Washington, D. C.: U.S. Government Printing
Office, 1918), Table 1, p. 88.

It will be observed from the above comparison that the difference in the percentages for communities of specified sizes increases
as the size of the community increases, the only exception being the
case of communities with more than 500, 000 population. The largest
observed difference is for communities between 100, 000 and 500, 000
in population. The magnitude of this observed difference is owing
to the influence of individuals born and reared in the District of Columbia which, at the time of the 1910 Census, was included in this
class.

When the states in which the subjects were born are classified into regions according to the scheme used by the Bureau of the
Census, it is observed that a larger proportion of the subjects, as
compared with the total Negro population, lived in the North in 1910.
This comparison, shown below, considers only those subjects born
in this country. (Fifteen respondents, or five percent, of our sample, as compared with 0.4 percent of the total Negro population in
1910,[18] were foreign born. All of the foreign-born subjects in the
present study came from the West Indies, while an overwhelming
proportion of those in the total population were born in that area.)

Table 2

Region of Origin of Sample Population
and Total Negro Population, 1910

| | Percentage Living in Specified Region, 1910 | | |
Region	Sample	Total Negro Population*	Difference (in percent)
South	80.4	89.0	-8.6
North	18.2	10.5	+7.7
West	1.4	0.5	+0.9

* Data taken from: Bureau of the Census, Negro Population in the
United States, 1790-1915 (Washington, D. C.: Government Printing
Office, 1918), Table 3, p. 33

The higher proportion of subjects from the North in the sample helps to explain its more urban character when compared with the
1910 Negro population. Negroes in the North in 1910 were located
predominantly in urban places, with 77.4 percent of the population
so classified. In contrast, Negroes in the South were located mainly
in rural areas, with only 21.2 percent being classified as urban.[19]

The Community

Only a brief word is necessary regarding the community in which the study was conducted, as no attempt is made to project the significance of the results beyond the particular area. As the seat of the Federal Government and a point just north of the slave states of the upper South, the District of Columbia attracted a relatively large number of Negroes during the Ante-Bellum period. This number included former slaves who escaped from the South through the underground railroad and manumitted persons who sought a more secure environment elsewhere. The Negro population of the District was enumerated as 14,316 in 1860,[20] and there have been significant increases in its number each decade since that date. In 1910, just prior to the great migrations, the 94,446 Negroes living in the District made it the largest Negro community in the country.[21] By 1950 the Negro population of the District had increased to 280,803 and constituted 35 percent of the total population for the area.[22] The Negro population of the District is thus the fifth largest Negro community in the United States, with only New York, Chicago, Philadelphia, and Detroit having a larger number of Negroes.[23]

Negroes in the District of Columbia have been employed largely in semiskilled and unskilled capacities and, recently, a rather large number of them have found employment in clerical occupations. The growth of the clerical group is owing largely to the demands of the Federal Government, as it expands, for persons possessing clerical skills, and to the increased willingness to employ Negroes with such skills. The sizeable Negro population of the District is able to and does support a relatively large corps of Negroes in the independent professions, while the traditionally segregated school system has, up to the present time, furnished employment to a substantial group of Negro teachers. One investigator, after examining the occupational statistics for communities in the North, South, and Border areas, notes that the occupational differentiation of the Negro population of the District of Columbia (and other Border cities as well) has not progressed as far as for cities in the North, but the professional and clerical groups in these cities are larger than those found in Southern cities. [24]

Howard University, established in 1867, is located in the District. It is the only Negro institution with a liberal arts college and most of the professional schools. Negroes in the District have had an excellent opportunity, therefore, for educational preparation for whatever professional field they wished to enter. It should be noted, moreover, that the District has a good public school system, dating back to 1862. It is not surprising that the community has more Negro college and professional graduates in proportion to total Negro population than is true for the country as a whole, or for Negroes in other urban areas. In 1950, for example, the percentage of Negroes twenty-five years of age and over in the District who were college graduates was more than twice as large as the comparable percentage for Negroes of this age category in other urban areas, and two-and-one-half times as large as the comparable percentage for the Negro population of the country as a whole. [25]

The presence of Howard University, with its professional schools of medicine, dentistry, pharmacy, law, architecture and engineering, music, social work, and religion, means in effect that students living in the District of Columbia who desire education for a professional career may secure it in their home community. The inclusion in our study of a sizeable number of persons born and reared in the District makes it possible to compare this group with

those born and reared in other areas in evaluating the accessibility
to education as a factor related to mobility. Certainly in few other
areas of the country may a Negro boy have the opportunity for an
advanced education at so low an expenditure available to him as the
presence of Howard University makes available to those living in
the District.

There are other features of the community which serve as
attractions to those in the professions. Freedmen's hospital, with
its 348 beds and 54 bassinets in the general hospital and a tubercu-
losis annex with 150 beds, offers a number of residencies and as-
sistant residencies to those who wish to qualify as medical specialists. In past years, to a greater extent than is true at present,
physicians wishing to qualify for specialty boards or who desired
advanced clinical training were inclined to remain in the community,
inasmuch as many white hospitals did not offer such opportunities to
Negro physicians. It is small wonder that of the 92 Negro physicians
who were diplomates of medical specialty boards in 1947, the largest number for any single city in the country, 26, were located in
the District. [26] The number had increased to 33 by 1950. [27]

In addition to the educational and training facilities mentioned
above, the community has had a long tradition of professional associations. The exclusion of Negro functionaries from white professional organizations led, inevitably, to the formation of voluntary
associations by the former. These associations appeared rather
early among the physicians and dentists. The Medico-Chirurgical
Society, organized in 1884, is the oldest Negro medical society in
the country. [28] The Robert T. Freeman Dental Society, founded in
1900 and named for the first Negro graduate in the field of dentistry,
is the oldest Negro dental society in the United States. [29] The

Washington Bar Association, the professional association of Negro
lawyers, appeared somewhat later, having been incorporated in
1925. Negro lawyers, however, met as a group for professional
reasons prior to the formal incorporation of the Bar Association.[30]

It is clear from the foregoing comments on the nature of the
community that the District of Columbia offers certain advantages
for the study of Negroes in the professions. These may be summarized as follows: (1) the presence of a substantial body of professional
functionaries in the major professions; (2) the presence of long professional tradition, as evidenced from the relatively early formation
of professional associations; (3) an occupational structure more
highly differentiated than that found in most Southern urban areas,
yet not so differentiated as that found in large Northern cities; and
(4) the presence of Howard University, which makes it possible to
use the Washington residents for comparing them with persons from
other areas in studying the factor of accessibility to education. The
assumption here is that those born and reared in the District may
secure a professional education in their home community, a condition
not available in many other communities in the country.

III.

THE OVERALL PATTERN OF MOBILITY:
OCCUPATIONAL ORIGINS AND INHERITANCE

In this chapter we are concerned with the amount of vertical
mobility demonstrated by our respondents and with the direction of
that mobility. By vertical mobility is meant simply the movement
of a son out of the father's occupational class, toward an adjudged
"higher" or "lower" level. Table 3 shows the distribution of our respondents' fathers according to their occupational levels.

The most striking fact demonstrated by Table 3 is that more
than one-third of the fathers of our respondents were engaged in professional occupations. This is true for each of the groups studied,
except for the dentists among whom fathers in the professional group
constituted approximately one-quarter of the total. The next largest
group of fathers is represented by the clerical group; between one-
sixth and one-seventh of all fathers were identified with that occupational class. Fathers in the proprietor and service workers groups
constituted each about one-eighth of the total number of fathers,
while the farming groups (owners and laborers) together made up
about one-twelfth of all fathers. Operators or semiskilled workers
represented about one-sixteenth of all fathers. The remaining fathers, 4 percent, were classified as unskilled workers.

It is sufficient at this point to observe that our respondents
have their occupational origins mainly in the white collar occupational
group--professional, proprietor, and clerical. These three occupational categories together account for almost three-fifths (59. 2 percent) of the fathers. Equally striking is the fact that at a time when

Table 3

Regular Occupation of Respondents' Fathers, for All Respondents
and for Each Professional Group, by Percent

Occupational Level of Father	No. of Cases	Percentage Distribution				
		All Classes	Physi-cians	Den-tists	Law-yers	Teach-ers
Professional	97	31.8	31.1	23.9	33.8	38.0
Proprietor	33	12.0	13.3	8.7	16.2	6.5
Clerical	45	15.4	16.7	17.4	13.2	14.1
Skilled	33	10.2	10.0	6.5	8.8	16.3
Farm owners	21	7.8	5.6	19.6	5.9	3.3
Semiskilled	18	6.2	1.1	4.3	14.7	5.4
Protective service	1	0.2	-	-	-	1.1
Service workers (except domestic and protective)	36	12.0	16.7	15.2	2.9	13.0
Farm laborers	1	0.4	1.1	-	-	-
Laborers (except farm)	11	4.0	4.4	4.3	4.4	2.2
Total	296*	100.0	100.0	100.0	100.0	100.0

* Based upon 296 fathers. There were four cases in which respondents did not know their fathers' occupation.

the Negro male labor force was heavily agricultural,[1] less than one-twelfth (8.2 percent) of the respondents' fathers were engaged in agricultural pursuits. The remainder of the fathers, about one-third (32.6 percent), were skilled and unskilled workers.

If now respecting occupations we compare the fathers of our respondents with the distribution of the married Negro male workers in 1910, the results of the comparison further support the observation that our respondents constitute a select group from the viewpoint of their occupational origins. Table 4 presents a comparison, using the method of expected cases, between the occupational distribution of our respondents' fathers and the married Negro male workers in 1910.[2]

Table 4

Comparison of Occupational Distribution of Respondents' Fathers
with Occupational Distribution of Married Negro Male Workers
16 Years of Age and Over in 1910, Using the Method of Expected Cases

Occupational Class of Worker	Estimated Number of Married Negro Males (1910)	Proportion of Labor Force	Distribution of Fathers		Ratio of Actual to Expected
				Based on Specific Rates	
			Actual	for 1910	
(A)	(B)	(C)	(D)	(E)	(F)
Professional	24,171	.012	97	3.5	27.71
Proprietor	21,976	.011	33	3.3	10.00
Clerical	20,655	.010	45	3.0	15.00
Skilled	72,428	.136	33	10.6	3.11
Farm owners	511,157	.251	21	74.3	.28
Semiskilled	123,751	.061	18	18.1	.99
Protective service	5,380	.003	1	0.9	1.11
Service (except domestic and protective)	122,442	.060	36	17.2	2.02
Farm laborers	643,360	.318	1	94.1	.11
Laborers (except farm)[a]	485,955	.238	11	70.4	.16
Total	2,034,275	1.000	296[b]	296.0	-

a Includes percentage for domestic service. None of our respondents'
fathers is included in that category.

b Four respondents did not know their fathers' occupations.

The comparison noted in Table 4 centers around column "F",
which should be interpreted in the following manner. If the occupational distribution of the fathers of our respondents were the same as
that of married Negro males in the labor force in 1910, then the expression of that fact would be represented by unity, or 1.00, for each
row of column "F". A ratio of less than 1.00 means that the fathers
of our respondents were under-represented in that occupational

category, while, conversely, a ratio greater than one signifies that
fathers were over-represented in that particular category.

The data of Table 4 strengthen the observation noted earlier,
namely, that our respondents come from a select group of fathers
with respect to the factor of occupation. It is clearly demonstrated
that the fathers of our respondents were greatly in excess of their
expected numbers for the white collar occupations: professional,
proprietor, and clerical. The greatest divergence from expectancy
occurred in the professional category, where the ratio of the actual
to expected value was almost twice that of the next largest ratio,
which occurred in the clerical group. Of equal importance is the
fact that the farming groups are under-represented, the ratio in
column "F" being twenty-eight hundredths (.28), about one-fourth
the expected number, for farm owners, and eleven hundredths (.11),
or one-ninth the expected number, for farm laborers. As a matter
of fact, farm laborers were the most under-represented group in the
comparison. Unskilled laborers and domestic servants were almost
as poorly under-represented as were farm laborers, the ratio for
the combined groups being sixteen-hundredths (.16). Protective service workers and semiskilled workers were represented in about the
proportion of expectancy, while the ratios for skilled workers and
service workers, other than domestic and protective, were above
unity.

The table demonstrates, then, that our respondents on the
whole came from fathers in the white collar occupations in excess of
the proportions which would be true were the occupational distribution
of their fathers the same as that of married Negro male workers in
1910. Conversely, they had fewer fathers than expected among the
manual workers and farmers, as shown by Table 5.

Table 5

Comparison of the Occupational Distribution of Respondents' Fathers
with the Occupational Distribution of Married Negro
Male Workers (1910), Classified into
White Collar, Blue Collar, and Farm Workers

Occupational Class	Estimated Number of Married Negro Male Workers (1910)	Proportion of Labor Force (1910)	Fathers		Ratio of Actual to Expected
			Actual Distribution	Expected Distribution	
(A)	(B)	(C)	(D)	(E)	(F)
White collar	66,802	.033	175	9.8	17.85
Blue collar	809,956	.398	99	117.8	.85
Farmers	1,157,517	.569	22	168.4	.13
Total	2,034,275	1.000	296	296.0	-

The tripartite division of occupations in the above table shows
clearly the tendency of our respondents to come from fathers in the
"higher" occupational groups and to have fewer fathers than expected
in the "lower" occupational groups. The middle group--the blue
collar workers--approaches unity to a greater extent than either of
the extremes, the under-representation of fathers for this group
being only fifteen-hundredths.

It will be remembered from the discussion of the sample
that our respondents represent a more highly urban group with respect to place of origin than did the Negro population as a whole at
the time of the birth of our respondents. Doubtless this factor ex-
plains much of the differences in the occupations of the respondents'
fathers and the occupations of married Negro male workers in 1910.
One sees immediately that differences in rural-urban distribution
between the two groups explain much of the under-representation of
farmers among the fathers of our respondents. Our comparison

would be improved if we could hold constant the factor of the rural-urban distribution for the two groups--all married Negro male workers and the fathers of our respondents. The limited number of cases in our sample does not make such an operation feasible. It is possible, however, to make one comparison, involving an urban group, which will refine somewhat the extent to which our respondents' fathers vary from their contemporary married Negro male workers with respect to occupation. It is possible to compare the fathers of all respondents born and reared in the District of Columbia and those migrating there before the age of sixteen with the married Negro male workers of the District for 1910. This comparison is presented in Table 6.

An examination of column "F" of Table 6 indicates the same general pattern shown by Table 4. Our sample contains more than the expected number of fathers in the professional, proprietor, and clerical groups. The only change from the results of Table 4 in over-representation or under-representation occurs for the skilled workers and service workers when the two tables are studied. Whereas these two groups were over-represented in the comparison of the total sample with all married Negro male workers, in the comparison involving only fathers of our respondents from the District of Columbia, they were under-represented. The position of the laborers group remains unchanged in both direction and magnitude. The most significant difference of the comparison of the results of Tables 4 and 6 is the reduction in the amount of over-representation for the professional, proprietor, and clerical groups in the latter table. Whereas in the comparison involving all fathers of our respondents and the married Negro male workers in 1910 the extent of

Table 6

Comparison of Occupational Distribution of Fathers of Respondents
Born and Reared in the District of Columbia and Those Migrating
There with All Married Negro Male Workers 16 Years of Age
and Over for the District of Columbia in 1910

Occupational Class[a]	Estimated Number of Married Negro Male Workers (1910)	Proportion of Labor Force	Respondents' Fathers		
			Actual Distribution	Theoretical Distribution	Ratio of Actual to Expected
(A)	(B)	(C)	(D)	(E)	(F)
Professional	357	.025	25	1.8	13.89
Proprietor	619	.042	8	3.0	2.67
Clerical	1,005	.069	18	4.9	3.67
Skilled	966	.066	4	4.8	0.85
Semiskilled	591	.041	3	2.9	1.03
Service, other	4,913	.337	8	23.7	0.33
Laborers, other than farm	6,126	.420	5	29.9	0.17
Total	14,577	1.000	71[b]	71.0	-

a Farmer owners, farm laborers, and protective service classes
not represented either in sample or in 1910 statistics.

b There were 72 cases for the District of Columbia, but in one case
the occupation of father was not known.

over-representation for the professional group is 27.71 times the
expected number, for the proprietor group 10.00 times expectancy,
and for the clerical group 15.00 times expectancy; for the District
comparison, fathers of our District respondents compared with all
married Negro male workers 16 years of age and over for the District,
the corresponding proportions are 13.89, 2.67, and 3.67 times their
expectancy values.

If now the occupations of the fathers of our respondents from
the District of Columbia are grouped into white collar and blue collar

classes and the comparison made with similar groupings for all married Negro male workers in the District for 1910, the over-representation of our fathers in the professional, proprietor, and clerical classes is again demonstrated; but, in this analysis, the magnitude or size of the over-representation is smaller than is shown by the comparison involving all sample fathers and all married Negro male workers for the United States as shown by Table 5. Table 7, following, presents these results.

Table 7

Comparison of the Occupational Distribution of the Fathers of Respondents from the District of Columbia with the Occupational Distribution of All Married Negro Male Workers 16 Years of Age and Over in the District of Columbia for 1910, Classified into White Collar and Blue Collar Classes

Occupational Class	Estimated Number of Married Negro Male Workers (1910)	Proportion of Labor Force	Actual Distri-bution	Theo-retical Distri-bution	Ratio of Actual to Expected
(A)	(B)	(C)	(D)	(E)	(F)
White collar	1,981	.136	51	9.66	5.28
Blue collar	12,596	.864	20	61.34	.33
Total	14,577	1.000	71	71.00	-

Comparisons with Other Studies of Mobility

Having demonstrated that our respondents had fathers whose occupational status was superior to that of the married Negro male workers who were their contemporaries, we may compare the level of occupational origin of these respondents with those of professional subjects reported in other studies of occupational mobility. Inasmuch as the studies with which comparisons are made do not all use the

same occupational groupings, it is necessary to make the comparisons in different series, accommodating our data to fit the occupational classification of the particular study or studies with which
our data are compared.

Our first comparison is with the study of Davidson and Anderson[3] and with the one directed by Richard Centers for the Princeton University Office of Population Research.[4] Both of these studies
have their data on occupations classified into the socio-economic
groupings worked out by Alba Edwards for the Bureau of the Census.[5]
The division of the "proprietor" group into "large business" and
"small business" in Centers' study constitutes the only change of
the Edwards scheme. The Centers study represents a cross-section
of the adult white male population of the United States; the Davidson
and Anderson study, conducted in San Jose, California, was based
primarily upon the white male population of that city, a little less
than one-quarter of the respondents being "Foreign-born" whites or
members of "Other Races." The data of the three studies are presented in Table 8.

Table 8

Comparison of Occupational Origins of Respondents with the
Occupational Origins of Professional Respondents in
Two Other Studies of Mobility

Name of Study	Percentage of Fathers on Specified Level						
	All Groups	Profes- sional	Propri- etor	Cler- ical	Skilled	Semi- skilled	Un- skilled
Present	100.0	31.8	19.8	15.4	10.4	10.2	12.4
Davidson and Anderson	99.9	9.6	61.4	9.1	9.1	5.6	5.1
Princeton	100.0	23.0	33.0[a]	13.0	21.0	5.0	5.0

a Includes both "Large Business" and "Small Business" as classified
by Centers. Does not include farmers, as none are reported by the
study.

It is easily recognized that our respondents more nearly approximate the professional respondents of the Princeton study with respect to occupational origins than they do those of the Davidson and Anderson study. This closer relationship to the Princeton study should be expected inasmuch as the latter study, as previously mentioned, was conducted on an urban population, and our respondents are highly urban. (It is not only the urban character of the two populations, but the size of the city as well which influences the levels of origin. [6]) A large percentage of our urban respondents come from large cities, between 100,000 and 500,000 in population. A large percentage of the urban population of the country is concentrated in metropolitan centers. The Davidson and Anderson study was done in a community of only 57,651 persons in 1930, [7] the nearest census year to the time of the investigation, a fact which affected the occupational pattern of the fathers, limiting particularly the opportunities afforded for employment in professional and white collar occupations.

It will be noted that respondents in our study have a larger percentage of fathers on the professional level than the Princeton study--31.8 percent as compared with 23.0 percent. A significantly larger proportion of the respondents in the Princeton study, however, have fathers who were in the proprietor class. Otherwise, the Princeton study shows about twice the percentage of fathers in the skilled worker group and only about one-half the percentage in the semiskilled and unskilled groups. It will be noted, further, that if we examine the respondents in the two studies having fathers at their level (professional) and at the two adjacent levels (proprietor and clerical), the percentages of fathers are found to be very nearly the same: 67 percent for the present study and 69.0 percent for the Princeton study. [8] The conclusion may be drawn from this comparison that our respondents come in greater proportions of fathers who are professional, semiskilled, and unskilled workers, while the professional respondents of the Princeton study have a larger percentage of fathers whose occupations are in the proprietor and skilled worker groups. The percentages of fathers in the clerical group were more nearly the same for the two studies than for any of the other occupational classes.

In contrast to our study, the largest percentage of fathers in the Davidson and Anderson study is in the proprietor class; more than three-fifths of the fathers of professional respondents in San Jose were in this occupational class. This percentage is three times the percentage of fathers in this class for our respondents. In every other occupational category, however, there is a smaller percentage of fathers than is true for our study. The most significant difference among the "other-than-proprietor" categories for the two studies is for the professional group. More than three times as many fathers in our study as compared with Davidson and Anderson's were in this occupational class. And finally, whereas four-fifths of the professional respondents in San Jose had fathers either on the professional level or the adjacent levels of proprietors and clerks, the proportion for our study, as noted above, was only two-thirds, a difference owing almost exclusively to the concentration of fathers in the Davidson and Anderson study in the proprietor group.

Certain tentative conclusions may be drawn from the comparisons of our study with those discussed in the preceding paragraphs.[9] These may be summarized in the following manner. Professional respondents on the whole in the studies cited tend to come more frequently from higher occupational levels, if we consider the subjects' level (professional) and the two adjacent ones (proprietor and clerical) as higher. Within these three levels--when they are considered sep-arately, that is--some differences are found. The subjects of our study come more often from families in which the father was a pro-fessional worker, while for the other studies, professional subjects come more frequently from families in which the father's occupation was in the proprietor group. Lastly, our respondents show a greater tendency to come from families with fathers occupied in semiskilled and unskilled work. These tentative formulations may be tested in the comparison made below, where our respondents are contrasted with those included in the survey made by North and Hatt for the National Opinion Research Center. [10]

The study conducted for the National Opinion Research Center by North and Hatt (hereafter referred to as NORC) considered a cross-section of the American population, asking a sample popula-tion questions relative to job evaluations. The study included also materials on mobility and classified occupations into basically the occupational classifications of the labor force statistics of the Six-teenth Census. The occupational origins of professional workers in the NORC study, along with those of our respondents, are presented in Table 9.

Taking first the percentages of respondents for the two stud-ies whose fathers are professional, proprietor, and clerical workers, we note that the percentages are nearly the same: 58.2 percent for our respondents and 57.0 percent for the NORC respondents. The separation of the farm category from the proprietor group doubtless influences this result. It will be noticed that the farm group among the NORC fathers is twice the size of this group in our study. As in the other comparison, however, while the largest single percentage of our respondents have fathers who are professional workers, the

Table 9

Occupational Origins of Respondents of Present Study Compared with the
Occupational Origins of Professional Respondents in the
National Opinion Research Center's Survey

	Occupation of Father								
Name of Study	Profes-sional	Propri-etor	Cler-ical	Skilled	Semi-skilled	Serv-ice	Farm	Non-farm Labor	Don't Know
Present[a]	31.1	11.8	15.3	10.1	6.1	12.0	8.0	3.9	1.6
NORC	23.0	24.0	10.0	13.0	5.0	5.0	17.0	2.0	1.0

a This distribution varies a little from the one presented in the other comparison, since it is based on the entire 300 cases in the sample. Four cases formerly excluded from tabulations because the occupations of the fathers were not known have been added to the "Don't Know" category above.

largest single percentage of fathers in the NORC study is in the
proprietor group. At the bottom end of the groupings, from the
semiskilled group down, our respondents have larger percentages
of fathers in those occupational groups, the largest single difference being in the service group, where there are found nearly two-
and-à-half times the percentage of fathers for our respondents as
for those in the NORC study.

On the basis of the comparisons of our study with the three
other studies for which data on the occupational level of fathers are
available, it seems that the Negro professional workers of our study
have a larger percentage of fathers on the professional level, and
that professional workers among whites come more often from fathers in the proprietor group. Also, it appears that larger proportions of the present generation of Negro professionals come from
fathers engaged in semiskilled and unskilled occupations. In all of
the studies, including the present one, there is agreement that most
professional workers are drawn from families in which the fathers'
occupational level is professional, proprietor, or clerical. Differences within the white collar category, as points of origin for the
two groups, Negroes and whites, are a function of the opportunities
for mobility and the images which are developed with regard to possibilities for vertical mobility.

Generational Mobility

We may now examine the occupational distribution of our
respondents' grandfathers in order to gain further knowledge of the
background of our professional group. [11] It will be remembered that
these grandfathers reached their maturity shortly after the Emancipation. Table 10 presents the distribution of the paternal grandfathers
for the entire group and for each of the professional groups separately.

Table 10

Occupational Distribution of Respondents' Paternal Grandfathers for the Entire Group
and for Each Professional Group Shown Separately, by Percent

Occupational Level of Paternal Grandfather

Class of Respondent	Profes- sional (1)	Propri- etor (2)	Cler- ical (3)	Skilled (4)	Semi- skilled (5)	Farm Owner (6)	Service Pro- tective (7)	Service Other than Farm (8)	Laborers Farm (9)	Laborers Other (10)	Unknown (11)
All Groups	7.0	7.3	2.3	7.3	3.0	19.7	1.3	1.7	4.7	3.7	42.0
Physicians	5.6	3.4	3.4	12.1	-	21.1	3.4	-	2.2	4.4	44.4
Dentists	6.5	6.5	4.3	6.6	4.3	13.0	-	2.2	2.2	2.2	52.2
Lawyers	8.3	9.7	-	4.2	4.2	19.4	1.4	2.8	2.8	2.8	44.4
Teachers	7.6	9.8	2.2	5.4	4.3	21.8	-	2.2	9.8	-	37.0

The single most important fact presented by Table 10 is the number of cases in which the occupation of the paternal grandfather is not known. For the entire group, those not knowing their grandfather's occupation, as indicated in column 11, amount to 42 percent. This is not unusual in the case of a group with the type of family experiences which Negroes have had. Moreover, in other studies[12] also the fact is reported that respondents do not know their grandfathers' occupations in a substantial number of cases. This fact imposes some necessary caution upon the interpretation of the data.

Another fact which stands out strikingly in the table presented is that the paternal grandfathers were heavily identified with agriculture. It is significant that about one-fifth of the total group of grandfathers were owners of farms, while another 4.7 percent of them were farm laborers. Together, these two groups make up almost 42 percent of those paternal grandfathers for whom the factor of occupation is known and one-quarter of all paternal grandfathers. Doubtless a large proportion of those grandfathers for whom the occupation is reported as "Unknown" belongs with those classified in one or the other of the farm groups.

It is interesting to note that, according to the percentages shown in Table 10, grandfathers were found in the professional, proprietor, and skilled labor groups in almost identical proportions. These three occupational groups accounted for a little more than one-fifth of the occupations of the grandfathers. It should be pointed out, however, that some of the grandfathers in the proprietor group were building contractors and, in one sense--if viewed from the kind of skill involved, they would be placed with the skilled group and would thus raise the percentage of that category slightly above those of the professional and proprietor.

Three comments of a general nature seem warranted by the data on occupational distribution of paternal grandfathers. (1) The typical grandfather was likely to have been identified with agriculture or some type of skilled manual labor. (2) The weight of these two groups, farm and skilled labor, gives the group more blue collar workers than white collar workers. And (3), the paternal grandfather was likely to be at the top level of the occupational category in which he was found: a skilled worker rather than a semiskilled or unskilled one, a farm owner rather than a farm laborer.

For the sake of greater perspective on the occupational distribution of the paternal grandfathers of our respondents, we may compare their distribution with the distribution of paternal grandfathers of the professional respondents in the NORC survey. These two sets of data are presented by Table 11.

It will be observed that the percentage of grandfathers whose occupation is "Unknown" comprises a large proportion of the total number of grandfathers in the NORC study. The same condition was true of our sample, as previously pointed out. It is fair to observe, however, that the percentage for this category in the NORC study is only approximately one-half as large as the corresponding percentage for the present study. The concentration of so large a percentage of cases in the "Unknown" category has a marked effect on the distribution shown for other categories. However, it is feasible to point out some similarities and variations for the two sets of data.

The most striking fact to be noted is that the percentage of respondents of the NORC study whose grandfathers were in the professional and proprietor occupational classes is almost twice as large as the corresponding percentage for the present study. If only the grandfathers whose occupations are "Known" are considered, two points of

Table 11

Comparison of the Occupational Distribution of Respondents' Paternal Grandfathers
with Those of Professional Respondents in the NORC Survey

Percent of Paternal Grandfathers on Specified Level

Study	Profes-sional	Propri-etor	Cler-ical	Skilled	Semi-skilled	Farm	Serv-ice	Non-farm Labor	Unknown
Present	7.0	7.3	2.3	7.3	3.0	24.4[a]	3.0[b]	3.7	42.0
NORC[c]	12.0	13.0	3.0	7.0	7.0	36.0	1.0	1.0	20.0

a Both farm owners and farm laborers included in this group to accord with the NORC category.

b Includes our "Protective Service" group.

c Taken from North and Hatt, "Jobs and Occupations: A Popular Evaluation," in Logan Wilson and William Kolb, Sociological Analysis (New York: Harcourt, Brace and Co., 1949), p. 473.

similarity are shown by the distributions. The first is that the largest percentage of grandfathers for each group is concentrated in the "Farm" category. Secondly, it is observed that five-sixths of the grandfathers of the present sample and only slightly less than three-quarters of those in the NORC study were blue collar workers.

Occupational Transmission

The concept of occupational transmission has been used in two ways in the literature on occupational mobility. In one sense, it is used to refer to the amount of transmission which is found when sons enter the "same" occupation as the father. Thus, if a physician has several sons, each of whom becomes a physician, then the amount of transmission is 100 percent. In another sense, the concept has been used to refer to the transmission between one generation and another of the same socio-economic status, and not necessarily of the same occupation within the socio-economic category. Thus, if a skilled worker, a carpenter, for example, had several sons, one of whom becomes a brick mason, one a factory foreman, and one a plasterer, the percentage of transmission from father to sons is again 100 percent. The sons have followed the same general status as the father and hence have inherited his status, though not his specific occupation. It is in these two ways that occupational inheritance or transmission is discussed in our analysis of this factor. [13] It should be mentioned that inheritance is really the negative aspect of mobility; that is, where mobility is found to be high, inheritance or transmission will be low, and vice versa.

Inheritance of Specific Occupations

The inheritance of specific or identical occupations is so small that we, perforce, must concentrate on the second connotation

of occupational inheritance, namely, the inheritance of a particular
socio-economic status. So little of a tradition of the sons' following the father's specific occupation has been possible over the three
generations which are included in the experiences of this group, that
only passing attention is necessary.

There is only one instance, for example, where paternal
grandfather, father, and son have followed the same occupation, and
this occurs among the teachers. For no one of the other groups is
such a case found. The grandfathers (paternal) who were professional persons were almost wholly engaged in the ministry or in
teaching. It is possible, of course, that if data were available on
all of the sons of the paternal grandfathers--that is, on the male
siblings of our respondents' fathers as well as on the fathers, the
percentage of transmission from paternal grandfather to offspring
would be increased.

The amount of inheritance of the same occupation is somewhat
higher, though still not very high, when we consider only father and
son. Considering families only, the transmission is highest for the
teacher group. Only in 10 cases among our 92 teacher respondents
were the occupations of respondent and father the same, giving a
transmission percentage of 10.9. Table 12 shows the percentage of
transmission of identical occupation from father to son for each of
the professional groups included in the study.

If, now, instead of considering identical transmission by
families we consider the number of sons entering the father's occupation as a percentage of all the fathers' sons, the percentage transmission is even lower, as gained from Table 13.

These figures of identical transmission are lower than those
reported in other studies. Davidson and Anderson[14] report the

Table 12

Transmission of Identical Occupations from Father to Son
for All of the Professional Groups
and for Each Group Shown Separately

Professional Group	Number of Families	Number in Which Father and Son Have Identical Occupations	Percentage Transmission
Teacher	92	10	10.9
Dentist	46	1	2.2
Physician	90	5	5.6
Lawyer	68	5	7.4
All Groups	296*	21	7.1

* In four cases, occupation of father was not known.

Table 13

Respondents and Their Adult Siblings Having the Same Occupation
as Their Fathers, for All Professional Groups
and for Each Group Shown Separately

Professional Group	All Fathers	Number of Sons Gainfully Employed	Number of Sons Having Same Occupation as Father	Percentage Transmission
Teacher	92	239	15	6.3
Dentist	46	125	1	0.8
Physician	90	198	5	2.5
Lawyer	68	155	5	3.2
All Groups	296	717*	26	3.6

* There were 722 sons for the entire group, but in five cases the
occupations were not known.

percentage of "identical" transmission between father and son as
8. 3; while Sorokin[15] gives 10. 6 and 12. 7 percent for two separate
studies of transmission of occupation from father to son, and 26. 1
and 24. 5 percent for these studies when all gainfully employed sons
are considered. It will be noticed that when all sons are considered,
the percentage of occupational transmission in the studies reported
by Sorokin increases, while in our study the percentage of transmission decreases.

Sorokin has called attention to the fact that the percentage of
occupational transmission decreases if this factor is measured over
several generations and points to the Industrial Revolution, the growth
of the division of labor, increases in the means of transportation, and
horizontal mobility as factors in this change. [16] Our low transmission
percentage is owing chiefly to the fact that most of the professional
fathers of our respondents were concentrated in teaching and the ministry. These two professions account for 55 of the 97 professional
fathers, or approximately 57 percent of them. [17] Many of the sons
of those in teaching and the ministry have entered other professions,
remaining thus at their fathers' general socio-economic level, but
showing some horizontal mobility.

Transmission of Socio-Economic Status

We may now discuss the amount of transmission considering
only the inheritance of socio-economic status. We shall consider only
those occupations which were known for the paternal grandfathers, the
distribution formerly shown for the fathers, and the occupational distribution of all of the fathers' adult sons, respondents and their male
siblings. It is necessary to take all of the sons, for by taking only the
respondents as representatives of the sons' group, we doubtless have

a select son. The occupational distribution of grandfathers, fathers,
and fathers' adult sons are shown by Table 14. This table permits
us to make a generational comparison of the occupational distribution
of these three groups and an evaluation of the occupational shifting
which has occurred over time.

Table 14

Occupational Distribution of Paternal Grandfathers,
Fathers, and All Adults Sons, by Percent

Occupational Class	Percentage Distribution		
	Grandfathers*	Fathers	All Adult Sons
Professional	12.6	31.8	63.6
Proprietor	12.6	12.0	5.4
Clerical	3.5	15.4	9.8
Skilled	12.6	10.2	7.1
Semiskilled	5.2	6.2	3.8
Farm owners	33.9	7.8	1.7
Protective service	2.3	0.2	1.7
Service, other	2.9	12.0	3.6
Farm laborers	8.1	0.4	0.4
Laborers, other	6.3	4.0	2.8
Total	100.0	100.0	99.9

* Based on 174 cases for whom occupations are known.

The most significant changes noted in Table 14 are the heavy
increases in the professional group from one generation to another,
and the precipitous decline in the farm groups. Both of these are
doubtless related to the urbanization of the Negro population. As
sons have moved to the city, the percentage of persons in agricultural
occupations has declined, and these sons, many of them at least,
have found opportunities in professional fields as Negro urban communities developed. Beyond this, we may say that in general there

has been an increase in white collar workers, although in the proprietor group there has been a decline over the period noted above. There has been also a decline among skilled workers. A clearer picture of these changes is gained from Table 15.

Table 15

Percentage Distribution of the Occupations of Paternal Grandfathers, Fathers, and All Adult Sons Classified into White Collar, Blue Collar, and Farm Groups, and Percentage Distribution in These Groups from One Generation to Another

Occupational Class	Percentage Distribution			Percentage Difference	
	Paternal Grand-father	Father	All Adult Sons	Father and Grandfather	All Adult Sons and Father
(1)	(2)	(3)	(4)	(5)	(6)
White collar	28. 7	59. 2	78. 8	+30. 5	+19. 6
Blue collar	29. 3	32. 6	19. 0	+ 3. 3	-13. 6
Farm	42. 0	8. 2	2. 1	-33. 8	- 6. 1
All Groups	100. 0	100. 0	99. 9	-	-

It will be noticed from columns 5 and 6 of Table 15 that the most widespread shifting in occupational groups occurred in the generation between grandfather and father, with the decline in agricultural occupations and the increase in white collar occupations being almost equal in magnitude and constituting the most significant changes. The rather heavy entrance into white collar occupations continued for the sons' generation, in which further declines in manual workers and farmers are noted. But it must be remembered that upward mobility demonstrated by the sons is almost wholly toward the professions as witnessed by the decline in both the proprietor and clerical groups when comparison is made with their fathers' occupations.

That the trend toward the professions noted in the generational picture above continues is gained from data on the sons of our
respondents, who represent a fourth generation. Our data on these
sons are limited inasmuch as the average age of our respondents is
only forty-five and not many have sons who are old enough to have
completed their training. Our 300 respondents have 34 sons who are
gainfully employed. Of these, 21, or 61.76 percent, have entered
professional occupations. Two others are proprietors, and seven are
engaged in clerical occupations. The total percentage entering white
collar occupations is thus 88.2. Less than one-fifth of the sons of
our respondents, then, have become blue collar workers.

We may now summarize the findings of this section. Our
respondents come from families in which the occupations of their
fathers are superior to those of the married Negro male workers who
were their contemporaries. Though the superiority of the fathers is
owing in part to the fact that they were more urban than the Negro
population as a whole, it is suggested by our findings on the District
of Columbia group that even when differences in areal distribution
are considered and urbanization held constant, the fathers' occupations are still "superior" to those of married Negro male workers.
The fathers were largely white collar workers, about three-fifths
of them, and the largest single concentration was found in professional occupations, nearly a third of them.

The occupational origins of this group resemble the pattern
found for other professional groups. Most of the sons who enter
professional occupations have fathers in white collar occupations,
so that the general theory that father's occupation is associated with
the chance of a son's attaining a higher-level occupation, inasmuch
as one does not move a great distance from his father's occupational
level, is found to hold in this study. Unlike other groups, our

professional respondents do not come chiefly from proprietor fathers, but rather from fathers employed in professional occupations. This peculiarity results from differences in the occupational structure of Negroes and whites. Negroes are not found heavily concentrated in the proprietor group; their occupational orientation at the upper levels has been toward professional fields. On the other hand, the world of business and market relations in general has been inviting to whites. Many fathers of our respondents might well have gone into business enterprises had the occupational value system under which they came to maturity been the same as that of the dominant group. We must believe, then, that the influence of the opportunities relating to occupations and the reality of the experiences encountered in the Negro community focussed many of the fathers on professional goals. It is thus that a heavier contribution to our professional sons is made by professional fathers than is the case among other groups studied.

There is little transmission of "identical" occupations from father to son, owing chiefly to the short history of the Negro group under freedom and to shifts in occupations. . This is particularly true of the grandfather-to-father transmission. Though our respondents had a considerable percentage of their fathers engaged in professional occupations, these fathers were mainly concentrated in teaching and the ministry. We find, then, a considerable shifting on the professional level, so that the transmission from father to son, as regards identical occupation, is low.

There is somewhat more inheritance of socio-economic status. Our first generation representatives, the grandfathers, were heavily concentrated in agricultural work. The fathers of our respondents were found in largest percentage in the professions, and our respondents and their brothers are concentrated to an even greater extent in the professions. It is suggested that the sons of our respondents will enter professional occupations to a greater extent than did their ancestors. Thus, it appears that over a period of slightly more than three generations a pattern of transmission of professional status has evolved. The development of a substantial professional structure occurred mainly in the father's generation, so that the transmission from father to son is greater than from grandfather to father.

Finally, it should be observed that the heavy concentration of fathers and sons in the professional occupations, as they become vertically mobile, shows the narrow confines of the occupational structure of the Negroes, particularly at the higher levels. In the grandfather's generation, for example, the percentages entering business and the professions are nearly equal, and each of these occupational categories claimed a higher percentage of the grandfathers than did clerical work. In both the fathers' and sons' generations there is a decline in the percentages entering business and an increase in the percentages entering clerical occupations. Yet, the percentage entering professional occupations for the fathers' generation is greater than the total of those entering both business and clerical occupations, and for the sons' generation more than four times as great.

IV

FACTORS ASSOCIATED WITH MOBILITY

In the past chapter we were concerned chiefly with the amount
and direction of the mobility demonstrated by our respondents. This
was done through an examination of the occupational backgrounds of
their fathers and grandfathers. In this chapter we shall discuss and
analyze some of the factors known to be associated with mobility.
The specific factors to which we shall give attention are: age, region
of origin, migration, family influence, and color.

Age as Related to Occupational Origin

It has been demonstrated already that the fathers of our respondents had a higher occupational status than the grandfathers, and
that this difference between fathers and grandfathers with respect to
occupational level had the effect of increasing the degree to which
socio-economic status was transmitted in the sons' generation as compared with the fathers'. The question may be raised whether our respondents show variations in their occupational origin when they are
classified into age groups so that the oldest ones may be compared
with the youngest ones. Accordingly, we have grouped the respondents into three age categories as shown in Table 16. These age
categories represent those born before the turn of the present century, the oldest group; those born between the turn of the century
and the beginning of the large-scale migration of Negroes during the
First World War, an intermediate group; and those born since that
period, our youngest group. The occupations of fathers have been

Table 16

Number and Percentage Distribution of Respondents Classified
according to Age of Respondent and Occupation of Father

| Occupational Level of Father | Age of Respondent | | | | | | |
| | Number | | | Percentage | | | |
	Total	Under 35	35-49	50 and Above	Total	Under 35	35-49	50 and Above
White collar	175	35	88	52	59.1	71.4	60.3	51.5
Blue collar	121	14	58	49	40.9	28.6	39.7	48.5
Total	296	49	146	101	100.0	100.0	100.0	100.0

classed into blue and white collar groups for the purpose of this comparison, the results of which show clearly that the status of the father
is highest for the youngest respondents. The fathers of those aged
fifty and above were almost equally divided between blue collar and
white collar workers; the other age groups show a preponderance of
white collar workers, the percentage increasing as age decreases.
When the entire table is tested for significance, the distribution is
found to be not significant. The only significant difference is found
between those under thirty-five and those aged fifty and above
($.05 < P < .01$).

These results are consistent with our findings on generational
mobility in which the tendency was noted for fathers to have a higher
occupational status than grandfathers. Since the range in age for the
entire group of respondents is from 80 years to 22 years, many of our
youngest respondents have grandfathers who are contemporaries of
the fathers of our oldest respondents. The most significant interpretation to be gained from the results on age, both for the generational
comparison presented in the previous chapter and for the data presented above, is that over a period of time those who enter professional
occupations come increasingly from fathers in the upper occupational
groups--professional, proprietor, and clerical.

It should be observed in passing that the youngest age group
was born during the period of marked social and economic advances
among Negroes. The migration of Negroes in substantial numbers
to cities of the South and, more particularly, to urban areas of the
North where a foothold was gained in industrial occupations, together
with the formation of large Negro communities which supported a
corps of professional workers in these urban areas, were characteristic of the period. In both Northern and Southern communities
marked advances in education were being made. These changes are
reflected in the higher occupational background of our youngest respondents as compared with the oldest respondents, the only significant difference with respect to age, it will be remembered. It appears,
then, that there is developing a more crystallized pattern of stratification in which the professional occupations studied have in recent
years recruited fewer persons of lower socio-economic origin than
was the case prior to the First World War.

Region of Origin

We may now turn attention to the regions in which the respondents were born to ascertain if there are differences in occupational origins with respect to this factor. Regions are classified, it
will be remembered, into North, South, and Border. Table 17 reveals
that in each region the respondents had a larger percentage of fathers
in the white collar group than in the blue collar category. The difference between the percentage of fathers in each of the two occupational
categories is smallest for the South, as one might expect, inasmuch
as the distributions reflect, in part at least, the economies of the
several regions and the Negro's ability to participate in the labor
force. Of interest to us, however, is the fact that these data tend to

Table 17

Occupational Origins of Respondents Classified according to
Region of Origin, by Number and Percent

Level of Father's Occupation	Number				Percent			
	Total	North	South	Border	Total	North	South	Border
White collar	163	27	73	63	58.6	56.3	53.1	67.0
Blue collar	115	21	63	31	41.4	43.7	46.9	33.0
Total	278*	48	136	94	100.0	100.0	100.0	100.0

* Fifteen West Indian respondents are not included. Does not include subjects from the West and those for whom father's occupation was not known.

support the proposition that most of the sons who become professional have fathers whose occupations are either on the professional level or on adjacent levels--proprietor or clerical. This finding should not obscure the importance of the fact that there is considerable recruitment of professional workers, as indicated by the data, from families in which the father was engaged in a blue collar occupation. In the South, for example, almost 47 percent of the respondents come from homes in which the father was a blue collar worker, while more than two-fifths of those from the North and one-third of those from the Border area have such an occupational background.

An overall test of the table reveals that no significant difference exists among the regions with respect to the level of occupational origin. When the different regions are compared with one another, however, the only significant finding results from a comparison of the South and the Border regions ($.05 < P < .01$). This moderately significant finding is owing doubtless to the economies of the two sections and to regional differences in Negro participation in the labor force. One notes, for example, that the Border area is heavily urban in character, and our respondents come from large cities within that region. [1] The number of fathers classed as farmers in the South would, of itself, make a heavy contribution to the difference noted. Moreover, opportunities for work in clerical occupations were much greater in the Border area than in the South during the first part of the century.

The District of Columbia. The District of Columbia, included in the Border area, as previously noted, presents a special case for testing. It is our opinion that boys reared in the District have an excellent opportunity for securing a professional education at home and, for this reason, we might expect to find a larger proportion of respondents of lower socio-economic origin from the District. Stated otherwise, if the father's occupation and income are related to the careers of his son, then father's occupation becomes less important in an area such as the District because of the accessibility to professional training at home. Howard University, with its professional schools, provides an opportunity for boys from the District to attend a professional school and live at home, thus eliminating some expenses which must be paid by those who come from other areas. [2]

When respondents from the District are compared with those from other regions with respect to level of occupational origin, the only significant finding is between the District and the South (.05 < P < .01). The percentage of District fathers whose occupations are classed as white collar is 71.2, a percentage which is larger than the comparable percentages for the South and North, and slightly higher than for the Border area as a whole. Here, again, the difference is doubtless owing to variations in the economy, but it is interesting to note than in the area where education is accessible to

the subjects, a larger percentage have their origins in the white
collar group than is true for any other area. There is a clear suggestion that factors other than the accessibility of educational facilities and money income operate to determine those who secure an
advanced education.

The West Indies. The number of respondents in our sample
from the West Indian Islands is so small--fifteen in number or 5 percent of the entire sample--that one cannot attach any real significance
to the findings of statistical tests of differences between this group
and those from other regions. Though a test reveals no significant
difference between our West Indian respondents and those from each
of the other regions, certain of the data on the socio-economic origins
of the West Indians are interesting and suggestive. The respondents
who were born in the West Indies come heavily from families in which
the father's occupation is in the white collar group (66 percent), but
in contrast to respondents from other areas, proprietor fathers out-
number fathers in professional occupations. As a matter of fact, fathers in proprietor occupations constitute the most numerous group
of fathers of our West Indian respondents. In this connection one important fact should be pointed out.

There has been a commonly shared belief among those who teach
West Indian students and those who work otherwise with West Indians
in professional occupations that a selective process operates to determine those persons of West Indian background who are able to secure
advanced educational training. The core of this belief is that those
who have been sufficiently fortunate to have the advantages of training
beyond that which is offered in the West Indies, where no facilities
for advanced training existed until recently, have been the sons and

daughters of the large landowners, the higher civil servants, and professional persons. The suggestion is offered by our data that such may well not be the case of those West Indians educated in the United States, inasmuch as the group most highly represented are the sons of small merchants. This is not to suggest that the sons of the landed group and of those engaged in government service and professional fields do not attend institutions of higher education. It does appear, however, that the sons of persons of affluence and power in the West Indies are more likely to attend graduate and professional schools in England and Canada, or on the European Continent, while those who attend colleges and universities in the United States represent a somewhat different social and economic stratum.[3] This fact has an influence, it appears, on the careers of West Indian respondents which makes for a different career pattern from those of our respondents from the United States, as pointed out in Chapter VI.

Migration. The discussion of regions thus far has considered only the place of origin or birth of the respondents. Many of our respondents' parents lived in two or more communities during the period of the respondents' youth. It is necessary, therefore, to compare those whose parents had changed residence one or more times before the respondents went to college with those whose families remained stationary.[4] The comparison is made respecting the level of father's occupation. Two-fifths of the families of all respondents had changed their place of residence one or more times before the respondent reached the age of sixteen. When the occupational level of the fathers of those who did not migrate is compared with the occupational level of the fathers of the migrant respondents, no significant difference is found between the two. When, however, the

occupational level of those who fathers moved from the South to the
Border and Northern areas is compared with that of those not showing a history of migration, a moderately significant difference is
found to exist $(.05 < P < .01)$, with the migrant respondents having
a larger number of fathers in the white collar group. This difference is a result of greater employment opportunities in the white
collar occupations in the North and Border areas and provides re-
inforcing evidence for our interpretation regarding the difference
between the Border and South with respect to level of occupational
origin. A comparison of those who moved to the North and Border
areas with those migrating elsewhere, either within the North or
within the South, reveals no significant differences.

Occupations of Sons

Thus far we have been discussing regional variations from
the viewpoint of occupational origins of respondents; in other words,
we have been looking backward from son to father. It is possible
to view mobility in still another way, namely, by looking forward
from the father's occupational level to those entered by his sons. In
making the analysis of the occupations entered by the sons, only the
adult male siblings of the respondents are considered. By taking
only the adult male siblings we doubtless get a more accurate measure of the amount of mobility experienced, for the respondents are
all professional persons and represent a highly select group among
the sons.[5] Table 18 presents the occupational distribution of the
siblings according to father's occupational level and region or origin.

It will be noted from the table that the siblings from the
South tend to enter professional occupations to a greater extent than
is true of those from the other two regions. (These differences are

Table 18

Occupational Distribution of All Adult Male Siblings according to
Region of Origin, by Percent

Occupational Level	North	South	Border	All areas
Professional	22.4	42.7	35.8	37.2
Proprietor	10.5	9.5	7.3	9.0
Clerical	19.4	13.3	22.9	17.1
Skilled	32.8	8.5	6.4	12.1
Semiskilled	6.0	3.8	11.9	6.5
Farm Owners	-	5.7	-	3.1
Protective Service	3.0	0.9	5.5	2.1
Other Service	3.0	8.1	6.4	6.7
Farm Laborers	-	1.4	-	0.8
Other Laborers	3.0	6.2	3.7	4.9
Total	100.1	100.1	99.9	100.0
White Collar	52.3	65.5	66.0	63.3
Blue Collar	47.7	34.5	34.0	36.7
Total	100.0	100.0	100.0	100.0
Number of Sons	67	211	109	387

statistically significant: the value of "t" is 3.4 for the observed
difference between South and North, and 2.1 for the observed difference between South and Border.) When one considers the percentages
entering white collar occupations, and not alone professional occupations, there is virtually no difference between the South and Border
regions. Both South and Border regions have a larger percentage of
siblings entering the white collar occupations than is the case of siblings from the North (the only significant difference for this latter
comparison is that found between South and North; "t" equals 2.0).
The percentage differences for the blue collar-white collar comparisons among the regions are not so great, then, as is the comparison

involving only those entering professional occupations. The narrowing of the difference between the South and the other regions in the former comparison is owing to the fact that in both the Border region and in the North there is a larger percentage of the siblings entering clerical occupations than is true for siblings from the Southern region.

It is clear from the foregoing analysis that the siblings from the Southern region, whose occupational origins were lowest, enter high prestige occupations in about the same proportion as is the case of siblings from the Border region and to a greater extent than is true of siblings from the North. Siblings from the South experience, in other words, greater vertical mobility than is true of those from the other two regions. The difference in mobility of Northern and Southern siblings is especially interesting and accords with information furnished by our interview data.

Respondents from the South testify to the strong desire on the part of their parents to have them enter high level occupations, especially professional occupations or those assuring a great amount of personal freedom. In numerous instances reported to us, parents left the South and moved to cities in the North and Border areas in order that their children might have the advantages of a good secondary school education as a foundation for college work. In some instances, the same objective was accomplished by having the children live with relatives in these areas for the specific purpose of attending high school. A good example of the concern of parents to have their children receive a good foundation and to move on to advanced training is furnished by one family which moved from a Kentucky community to Oberlin, Ohio, in order that the children might attend Oberlin College. The mother in the family was educated at Knoxville College, a church-related institution for Negroes sponsored by the Presbyterians.

There she came under the influence of white teachers, some of whom were graduates of Oberlin College. She was determined that her children would be well educated and persuaded her husband to move to the Ohio town when the older children were still quite young. She took in laundry work and her husband obtained a job as a cook at the college while the children were being educated. All five of their children were graduated from Oberlin College and later took advanced degrees. This example testifies not only to the strong influence exercised by the parents of Southern respondents, but also to the role of the white missionary teachers who encouraged many Southern boys remaining in the area to continue their studies.

In contrast to the experiences reported by respondents from the South are those related by respondents from the North, many of whom assert that their fathers tried to discourage them from continuing their formal education beyond the high school level. It was the feeling of their fathers that the sons should begin to support themselves after the completion of secondary school. This was especially true in those instances where the father was the proprietor of a small business and wished to have his son serve as a partner or employee.

The Influence of Father's Occupation

Most of the previous studies of occupational mobility have been concerned with the establishment of a relationship between father's occupation and the occupations entered by his sons. That there is a relationship of a positive nature between these two variables is now well established. The dominant finding in this connection is that most sons will be found either in the father's particular occupational class or in an occupation on a level which is considered adjacent thereto. For example, most sons of businessmen will follow some occupation

in the proprietor class or will be found in professional or clerical
work, which are considered as being levels adjacent to business.

In this section we are concerned not only with the relationship
between the occupations of fathers and sons, but also with the influence of father's occupation on the educational attainment of his sons.
We shall employ the adult male siblings of our respondents as representatives of the sons for the reasons advanced in the previous section.

Table 19 shows the occupations of all adult male siblings
classified according to the occupational level of their fathers. It will
be observed that there is a heavy movement of the siblings out of
their fathers' occupational class. It is only among the sons of fathers in professional occupations that a majority will be found in the
same occupational class as the father. The extent of movement out
of the father's particular class is further indicated by the fact that,
except for sons of skilled and unskilled workers, more sons will enter
professional occupations than will remain at their fathers' specific
level. Thus, for example, 51.0 and 50.0 percent, respectively, of
the sons of clerical and semiskilled fathers enter professional occupations, while only approximately one-quarter and one-eleventh, respectively, of the sons of such fathers remain on the father's occupational level. More than twice the percentage of sons of service workers remaining at their fathers' level will enter professional occupations. It is only among the skilled and unskilled classes that as many
sons will remain at their fathers' level as will enter professional occupations.

The pattern described in the preceding paragraph represents
a considerable amount of vertical mobility on the part of this group
of sons. The upward mobility for certain classes of sons may be
better viewed if we consider the percentage of sons having fathers

Table 19

Occupational Distribution of All Adult Male Siblings according to
Occupational Level of Fathers, by Percent

Level of Fathers' Occupation

Sons on Each Specified Level	Professional	Proprietor	Clerical	Skilled[a]	Semiskilled	Farm Owners	Other Service	Laborers[b]	All Groups
Professional	50.9	31.7	51.0	23.2	50.0	30.4	32.7	15.4	38.2
Proprietor	6.2	15.0	3.9	8.9	16.7	7.1	16.3	-	9.3
Clerical	17.0	13.3	23.5	25.0	16.7	8.9	12.2	15.4	16.6
Skilled	10.7	13.3	5.9	23.2	4.2	7.1	18.4	7.7	12.1
Semiskilled	2.7	8.3	3.9	10.7	8.3	1.8	4.1	38.4	6.4
Farm Owners	-	-	-	-	-	21.4	-	-	2.9
Protective Service	3.6	6.7	3.9	-	4.2	-	2.0	-	2.9
Service, Other	2.7	8.3	3.9	5.4	-	10.7	12.2	7.7	6.2
Farm Laborers	-	-	-	-	-	5.4	-	-	0.7
Laborers, Other	6.2	3.3	3.9	3.6	-	7.1	2.0	15.4	4.8
Total	100.0	99.9	99.9	100.0	100.1	99.9	99.9	100.0	100.1
Number of Sons	112	60	51	56	24	56	49	13	421[c]

a Includes two sons of fathers in Protective Service.
b Includes four sons of Farm Laborers.
c Does not include five sons whose fathers' occupations are unknown.

in the various occupational classes who enter occupations either on
their fathers' level or on adjacent levels as indicated by the following: professional, 74. 1; proprietor, 60. 0; clerical, 33. 3; skilled,.
58. 9; semiskilled, 12. 5; farm owners, 33. 9; service, 16. 2; laborers, 61. 5. It will be observed that for four of the occupational
classes--professional, proprietor, skilled, and laborer--a majority
of the sons will be found on the fathers' level and adjacent levels.
Sons of fathers of the other occupational classes, however, show a
tremendous movement away from their fathers' level and those adjacent thereto. Thus, two-thirds of the sons of clerks move away from
the levels considered, one-half of them moving into the professions.
And only one-eighth and one-seventh of the sons of semiskilled and
service workers, respectively, remain on the levels considered,
while not quite one-half of the sons of farm owners enter occupations
near to their fathers' level.

If we now consider the percentage of sons of various occupational classes who enter white collar occupations, we may again note
the upward mobility for certain of the sons, especially those whose
fathers are semiskilled and service workers. The percentage of
sons entering white collar occupations is as follows: professional,
74. 1; proprietor, 60. 0; clerical, 78. 4; skilled, 57. 1; semiskilled,
83. 4; farm owners, 30. 8; service, other, 61. 2; laborers, 30. 2

Only in the cases of skilled workers, farm owners, and laborers do less than three-fifths of the sons enter white collar occupations. More than three-fourths of the sons of clerical and semiskilled workers and approximately three-fourths of the sons of professional workers enter occupations in the white collar group.

The close relationship between certain types of jobs, especially those so-called higher level jobs, and educational attainment

would lead to an expectation of a relationship between father's occupational level and the educational attainment of his sons. There is, further, the fact that educational costs mount after one leaves the public school level, for even in our land-grant colleges and other public institutions the student has to pay fees and other nominal costs. Often room and board costs are expenses which must be met when the institution of learning is not located in the student's home town. There is, finally, the fact that parents who themselves have been the recipients of advanced training are prone to encourage their children to continue their educational training beyond that which is offered by the public school system. Often such parents are in a position to furnish substantial monetary assistance in addition to mere verbal encouragement and goal direction. It must not be overlooked, however, that some parents who have not been able to continue in school beyond the grade or high school level are anxious to have their children continue their education to advanced levels. In many cases, however, children of such parents have to stop school at the earliest possible age consistent with legal requirements to assist through their earnings in meeting the financial problems encountered by the family.

Table 20 presents data on the educational achievement of the sons (adult male siblings) of fathers at each occupational level. The average amount of education received by the entire group of sons, approximately fourteen and one-half years, may seem high, but it must be remembered that we are dealing with a rather select group. It will be noticed, however, that there is considerable variation in the median years of schooling for the various occupational categories. The range is from 17.3 years for the sons of fathers on the clerical level to 12.2 for the sons of skilled workers, a difference of 5.1 years of schooling.

Table 20

Educational Attainment of Adult Male Siblings and Median School Years Completed
by Siblings, according to Occupational Level of Father

Sons on Level Specified	Level of Father's Occupation								
	Profes-sional	Propri-etor	Cler-ical	Skilled[a]	Semi-skilled	Farm Owners	Other Service	Labor-ers[b]	Total
Grade School									
Under 7	-	-	-	7.1	-	19.6	4.1	15.4	4.5
7-8	6.3	6.7	5.9	17.9	-	16.1	8.2	-	9.0
High School									
9-11	6.3	15.0	7.8	12.5	8.3	1.8	18.4	23.1	10.0
12	14.4	25.0	19.6	19.6	20.8	17.9	14.3	23.1	18.3
College									
1-3 years	25.2	25.0	5.9	16.1	4.2	16.1	22.4	15.4	18.5
4 years	13.5	8.3	7.8	10.7	25.0	3.6	14.3	7.7	10.9
Graduate									
1-2 years	10.8	5.0	29.4	1.8	25.0	12.3	10.2	15.4	12.1
3-4 years	23.4	15.0	21.6	14.3	16.7	10.7	8.1	-	16.2
5 or more	-	-	2.0	-	-	1.7	-	-	0.5
Total	99.9	100.0	100.0	100.0	100.0	100.1	100.0	100.1	100.0
Median school years	15.8	13.5	17.3	12.2	16.7	12.9	14.9	12.5	14.4
Number of sons	111	60	51	56	24	56	49	13	420[c]

Notes at bottom of page 93, opposite.

It will be observed, further, that sons of clerical and semi-skilled workers have the highest average amounts of education. Sons of fathers in these two occupational groups, as pointed out previously, show the greatest tendency toward upward mobility. The sons of service workers, who also show a pronounced tendency toward upward mobility, average one-half year more of formal training than is the case of the entire group of sons. The educational attainment of sons of professional workers, as may be expected, is well above the median for the entire group of sons.

In contrast to the picture presented above, the sons of skilled workers, farm owners, and laborers are well below the median for the entire group. That the sons of proprietors fall below the median for the entire group in educational attainment is owing to the fact that such sons have the largest percentage stopping school after the completion of high school. There is the suggestion that the notion persists among businessmen that advanced training is not an indispensable prerequisite for a successful career. We have indicated in a previous section that many small businessmen in the North discouraged their sons from continuing their schooling beyond the high school level.

In an overall sense, this analysis of educational attainment indicates the close relationship which exists between educational training and occupational status.

---

a Includes two sons of fathers in Protective Service.
b Includes four sons of Farm Laborers.
c Does not include five sons whose fathers' occupations are unknown.

Financial Status of Parents

One of the crucial factors which determines the extent to which one is able to secure an advanced education, such as that demanded by a professional career, is the financial condition of one's parents. Financial status is, of course, related to occupation, so that in viewing the influence of this factor we are supplementing the knowledge gained from an investigation of the influence of father's occupational level on son's educational attainment.[6]

The median income of our respondents' parents was $2,280. Though there exist no comparable data on all Negro families for the period under study, beyond question this figure for our respondents' parents is far above that for the average Negro family at the time our respondents were ready for college, about 1922.[7] The range in income was from a high of $2,500 for the parents of physicians to $1,889 for the parents of lawyers. The incomes for the parents of dentists and teachers were $2,250 and $2,343, respectively. The income distribution of our respondents' parents is shown in Table 21.

Financial Support of Education

The importance of the family's economic status for the educational attainment of our respondents may be seen more clearly when we examine the manner in which the educational expenses of the respondents were met. Inasmuch as the analysis reveals a difference in the manner of financing undergraduate and graduate or professional training, these two are discussed separately.

In more than one-half of the cases, 56.0 percent, parents played a part in contributing substantial sums to the educational expenses of the respondent; the other 44.0 percent of the cases met

Table 21

Percentage Distribution of Parents of Respondents according to
Income Class, for All Groups and for Each Professional Group
Shown Separately

Income Class (Dollars)	Professional Group				
	Total	Physicians	Dentists	Lawyers	Teachers
Under $1,000	17.0	17.7	21.7	25.0	7.6
$1,000-$1,499	13.0	8.9	17.4	15.3	13.1
1,500- 1,999	12.3	12.2	4.3	12.5	16.3
2,000- 2,999	27.3	22.2	26.1	20.8	38.0
3,000- 3,999	14.7	18.9	19.6	9.7	12.0
4,000- 4,999	5.3	7.8	-	5.6	5.4
5,000- 7,499	4.7	6.6	4.3	5.6	2.2
7,500- 9,999	1.7	1.1	-	1.4	3.2
10,000 and over	2.7	3.3	-	4.2	2.2
Not given	1.3	1.3	6.5	-	-
Total	100.0	100.0	99.9	100.1	100.0
Median	$2,280.49	2,500.00	2,250.00	1,888.89	2,342.86
Mean	2,736.49	2,971.91	2,209.31	2,677.08	2,801.63

their expenses through their own earnings, through scholarship or
fellowship aid, or by a combination of sources. In two-fifths (46.3
percent) of all cases, parents contributed more than half of the expenses for the undergraduate education of our respondents. (The complete table on the methods of financing both undergraduate and graduate
or professional training appears in Appendix "C".) A larger percentage of the oldest respondents, as compared with the youngest group,
was responsible for their undergraduate expenses; it appears that
over time parents have made a heavier contribution to the expenses
at the undergraduate level, as shown by Table 22. Whereas for the
oldest respondents (fifty and over) and for those between the ages of

thirty-five and fifty the expenses were paid most often from the
respondents' earnings or from some other source, for the youngest
group (under thirty-five) parents contributed more than one-half of
the expenses in almost two-thirds of the cases. The degree to which
there is an increased tendency on the part of parents to support the
undergraduate education of the respondents is evidenced when the
distributions of Table 22 are tested for significance; the difference
between the parental support furnished those under 35 and those 35
to 49 is moderately significant (.05 < P < .01), while the difference
between those under 35 and those 50 years of age and over is highly
significant (P > .01).

The older respondents, as far as undergraduate education is
concerned, may be said to represent a "self-made" group. Though
parents may have been willing to support education, there was

Table 22

Chief Source of Income from Which Undergraduate Expenses
Were Paid, according to Age Group

Source of Income[a]	Age Group							
	Number				Percent			
	Total	Under 35	35-49	50 and Above	Total	Under 35	35-49	50 and Above
Parents	131	32	67	32	46.3	65.3	45.3	37.2
Other	152	17	81	54	53.7	34.7	54.7	62.8
Total	283[b]	49	148	86	100.0	100.0	100.0	100.0

a The totals have been arrived at by apportioning combination cases
to one or the other category in accordance with the proportion of expenses contributed. For example, for those respondents whose
expenses were met equally by parents and own earnings, one-half
of the total number of such cases is assigned to each group.

b In seventeen cases, the respondents did not attend college.

doubtless an inability to do so. Our younger respondents, however,
come from families in which the father has a higher occupational
status, and with this there goes evidently an interest in and an ability
to contribute larger sums toward the expenses connected with the
attainment of the respondent's first degree. Here we see clearly the
relationship between higher occupational level and the support of education.

The expenses of graduate and professional training are met
very largely from sources other than the respondents' parents. In
only one-quarter of the cases were parents responsible for more than
one-half of the educational expenses of the respondents at this level.
For the most part, the costs of advanced training were met from the
respondents' own earnings, this being true in more than one-half of
the cases. Scholarships and fellowships played a more significant
part in the financing of graduate and professional education than was
true of undergraduate training. This pattern of financing educational
training beyond the undergraduate degree has not changed significantly
with time. Though the youngest respondents receive somewhat more
assistance from parents than do the oldest respondents for advanced
education, the differences are not statistically significant. It appears,
then, that as one prepares for a career the costs of the undergraduate education are met almost equally from parental contributions and
from one's own earnings and other sources. But advanced training
is more the responsibility of the respondent. It should be added that
when the professional groups studied are compared with one another
some interesting differences appear. Since we are concerned only
with the overall pattern in this chapter, it is enough to indicate at
this point that the greatest difference lies in the significantly heavier
contribution of parents to the educational expenses of physicians as

compared with their contributions to meeting the expenses of the
other professional respondents, a consideration which will be given
attention in the following chapter.

There is one further fact which should be noted in connection
with the financing of education at both the undergraduate and graduate or professional levels. Parents of Southern respondents contribute less to the cost of training at both of the levels, as shown in
Table 23. The only significant difference existing between regions
with respect to this factor is that existing between the South and
Border regions which is found to be significant at the . 01 percent
level for both undergraduate and graduate or professional training.
This is the result very largely of the fact that students in the District
of Columbia, the largest group included in the Border area, are able
to live at home and thus have fewer expenses connected with non-
academic costs. It is for this reason that we have argued that the
possibilities for sons of families of lower socio-economic status to
secure an advanced education should be greater in the District of
Columbia than elsewhere.

Table 23

Contributions to the Undergraduate and Graduate Expenses of
Respondents, according to Region and Source of Contribution,
by Percent

Source of Contri- bution[a]	Undergraduate				Graduate or Professional			
	Total	North	South	Border	Total	North	South	Border
Parents	46. 3	44. 9	39. 5	59. 1	24. 0	28. 6	16. 1	34. 7
Other[b]	53. 7	55. 1	60. 5	40. 9	76. 0	71. 4	83. 9	65. 3
Total	100. 0	100. 0	100. 0	100. 0	100. 0	100. 0	100. 0	100. 0

a One-half of the total expenses must be contributed by source.

b Includes "Own Earnings," Scholarships, etc.

The pattern of support for West Indians is much the same as for respondents from the United States as a whole, with parents contributing more to the undergraduate expenses than to the costs of graduate and professional training. West Indians receive even less parental support than do respondents from any other region, however.

The relationship between financial status of parents and the amount of education received may be clearly seen if we consider the number of school years completed by the adult male siblings, according to the income levels of their fathers. Table 24 presents these data. It will be seen that the median years of schooling completed by the entire group is approximately fourteen and one-half years. The lowest income category, under $1,499, falls below the median, while the highest income category, $5,000 and above, is almost two years above the median. The difference in educational attainment for sons of the lowest and highest income categories is more than three years. These differences are rather considerable when it is remembered that we are dealing with a rather select group in which the lowest income category is doubtless superior to the general economic level of the average Negro family of the period. These data show that even within a select group, the amount of schooling received increases as family income increases.

Inasmuch as parental income has an influence on the amount of education received by the adult male siblings, it influences also the occupations which are followed by the group. This follows from the fact that for many jobs education is an indispensable prerequisite. We may, therefore, look at the relationship which exists between these two factors of education and income as shown in Table 25.

It is evident that as family income increases the tendency of sons to enter professional occupations in particular and the white

Table 24

Percentage of Adult Male Siblings Attaining Each Specified Level
of Schooling and Median Years of Schooling Completed by Siblings,
According to Income Level of Father

Sons on Level Specified	Income Class of Father				All Classes
	Under $1,499	$1,500-$2,999	$3,000-$4,999	$5,000 and over	
Grade School					
Less than 8 years	8.2	2.4	4.7	-	4.6
8 years	13.4	9.0	3.5	-	8.8
High School					
1 to 3 years	10.5	9.6	10.5	8.3	10.0
4 years	17.2	20.3	17.4	8.3	18.0
College					
1 to 3 years	16.4	18.6	16.3	25.0	17.8
4 years	8.2	12.6	14.0	12.5	11.4
Professional					
1 to 2 years	13.4	10.8	11.6	20.8	12.4
3 or more years	12.7	16.8	22.1	25.0	17.0
Total	100.0	100.1	100.1	99.9	100.0
Median years completed	13.09	13.94	14.40	16.38	14.50
Number of Sons	134	167	86	24	411

collar occupations in general is more pronounced. Sons who come
from families with incomes of $5,000 and above are well above the
averages of the entire group in the percentage entering professional
and white collar occupations. Sons of families in the lowest income
category are well below the averages, and those in the income category $3,000 to $4,999 approximate the averages. The most significant fact of the table, however, is the consistent increase in the
number of sons entering high level occupations with each increase
in family income. Even in the framework within which we are

Table 25

Percentage Distribution of the Occupations of All Adult Male Siblings
According to Income Level of Father, and Percentage Entering
White Collar, Blue Collar, and Farm Occupations

Occupational Level	Income Level of Father				All Classes
	Under $1,499	$1,500-$2,999	$3,000-$4,999	$5,000 and over	
Professional	31.3	38.9	46.5	50.0	38.7
Proprietor	19.7	8.4	7.0	16.7	9.0
Clerical	15.7	18.0	19.8	8.3	17.0
Skilled	9.7	11.4	17.4	8.3	11.9
Semiskilled	8.2	7.2	2.3	4.2	6.3
Farm Owners	7.5	1.2	-	-	2.9
Protective service	-	4.2	4.7	4.2	2.9
Other service	10.5	6.0	-	4.2	6.1
Farm Laborers	0.7	0.6	-	-	0.5
Other Laborers	6.7	4.2	2.3	4.2	4.6
Total	100.0	100.1	100.0	100.0	99.9
White Collar	56.7	65.3	73.3	75.0	64.7
Blue Collar	35.1	32.9	26.7	25.0	31.8
Farm	8.2	1.8	-	-	3.4
Total	100.0	100.0	100.0	100.0	99.9
Number of Siblings	134	167	86	24	411

operating--a select and superior group--it is evident that the ability
of a son to enter a high level occupation bears a relationship to the
income of his family of origin.

Educational Background of Respondents' Parents

The formal educational training of our respondents' parents
was far superior to that of the Negro population as a whole at the
time of our respondents' mean year of birth.[8] The fathers completed
an average of 11.3 years of schooling, while the mothers had

completed 12.0 years of formal training. The educational level of the fathers in this study is about the same as that reported for the fathers of white professional workers in another study, in which the fathers averaged eleven years of formal schooling.[9]

One notes from the complete tables on the educational distribution of the fathers and mothers, shown in Appendix "C", the homogeneity of level for each of the professional groups studied. The fathers of dentists, lawyers, and teachers each had an average of four years of high school education, while the physicians' fathers had slightly less, an average of nine years of schooling. The mothers of each of the four professional groups had twelve years of schooling. With regard to regions, little variation is found. The fathers living in the Border area and in the South had an average of twelve years of schooling, while the fathers of our Northern respondents had an average of nine years. West Indian fathers enjoyed ten years of formal training. These variations were not statistically significant.

The most significant variation in the educational background of our respondents is the change in the fathers' educational level with the age of the respondent. Table 26 shows the distribution of fathers according to educational level, classified according to the ages of their respondent sons. It will be noted that the average amount of schooling increases as age of respondent decreases. Whereas the fathers of the oldest respondents had an average of one year of high school education, the fathers of those between the ages of thirty-five and fifty had the twelve years of schooling, while the fathers of the youngest respondents, under thirty-five, had the equivalent of two years of college work.

Table 26

Educational Attainment of Fathers According to Age of Respondent,
by Percent

Years of Schooling Completed by Father	Age of Son			Total
	Under 35	35-49	50 and Over	
Grade School				
None	2.1	4.0	24.0	10.2
1-4 years	4.2	4.0	6.2	4.8
5-6 years	2.1	9.4	4.2	6.5
7-8 years	18.7	22.8	14.6	19.5
High School				
1-3 years	2.1	8.1	4.2	5.8
4 years	16.7	12.8	9.4	12.3
College				
1-3 years	12.5	16.1	13.5	14.7
4 years	12.5	7.4	10.4	9.2
Graduate School				
1-2 years	16.7	6.0	7.3	8.2
3 or more years	12.5	9.5	6.2	8.8
Total	100.1	100.0	100.0	100.0
Median Number of Years*	14	12	9	12

* Medians calculated by single years.

If we take only the oldest and youngest respondents and note
the distribution of their fathers according to the amounts of schooling
received, we note that the difference of five years between the two
in average amount of schooling is accounted for largely in two ways.
There is in the first instance a sharp reduction in the percentage of
fathers in the two groups who were illiterate. Whereas one-quarter
(24.0 percent) of the fathers of the oldest respondents had no formal
training, only 2 percent of the fathers of the youngest group were so
classified. The dramatic nature of this reduction is better grasped

if we think of the change as being from one in four fathers illiterate for the oldest group to one in fifty for the youngest group. The second factor which accounts for the difference in the average a- mount of education for the two groups is the variation in the per- centage of fathers having graduate or professional training. The percentage of fathers having graduate or professional training for the youngest group is slightly more than twice as large as the per- centage having such training among the fathers of the oldest re- spondents--29.2 percent as compared with 13.5 percent. If it is remembered that our respondents had an average of nineteen years of formal training and their siblings an average of fourteen years, it is seen that as the age of son decreases there is an increase in the educational level of the father. In other words, the difference between the educational attainment of father and son is less for the youngest respondents than for the oldest respondents. This finding accords with our previous result on the occupational level of father according to age of son in which it was observed that the occupational level of father increased as the age of son decreased. It is now clear that sons experience less upward mobility from the father's occupational and educational levels with time, which, in other words, means that a more crystallized stratification pattern is developing among members of the Negro group.

The Role of Color

In dealing with the mobility of the Negro group we are faced with the study of one factor which studies of mobility of other groups do not have to consider. Skin color has played an important part in the experiences of the Negro group. Historically, mulattoes enjoyed an advantage during the slave period; many of them enjoyed the favor

of the masters, whose bastard children they often were. The con-
tacts and opportunities which they enjoyed as house servants and in
other preferred jobs on the plantation, and the opportunities for formal learning permitted in some cases by their owners, gave them a
start in life beyond that of the field slaves. Moreover, as a result
of sentiment or meritorious service, many of the mulattoes were
freed prior to the Emancipation. As free Negroes they enjoyed opportunities for learning, informally, not available to the average
slave. The post-Civil War period found this mulatto group equipped
to serve as leaders of the freedmen. The role of the mulatto has
been described at greatest length by Reuter, from whose writing we
quote, particularly for the bearing his exposition has on Negroes in
professional fields.

> The mulattoes, at all times in the history of the Negro in
> America, have been the superior individuals of the race. Of
> the score or so of men of first-rate ability which the race
> has produced, not more than two at the most were Negroes
> of pure blood. Of the two hundred or so who have made the
> most noteworthy success in a business or professional way
> all, with less than a dozen exceptions, are Negroes of mixed
> blood. Of some two hundred and forty-six persons, presum-
> ably the most successful and the best known men the race
> has produced, at least thirteen-fourteenths of them are men
> of mixed blood. Of the list of six hundred and twenty-seven
> names of persons compiled from the historical and biograph-
> ical literature and including men of a distinctly lesser degree
> of note, only about one-ninth were even of approximately
> pure blood. The same condition was found to prevail in the
> examination of compilations of the leading men in the various
> professional and semiprofessional pursuits; the professional
> men of the race are nearly all mulattoes as are the men who
> have succeeded in some form of artistic or semi-artistic
> endeavor...It was further found that by taking a large num-
> ber of cases from any profession or pursuit and consequently
> tapping lower ranges of ability and success, the ratio of black
> men to mulattoes was increased. The higher the standard

of success, the lower the per cent of full-blooded Negroes.
This was the case as between different professions and within
the ranks of the same profession; the ministry had a much
higher per cent of full blooded Negroes than does the medical
or the teaching profession; the higher positions in all the professions have been reached by mulattoes, very seldom by
black Negroes. Speaking generally, the intellectual class of
the race is composed of mulattoes; a black man in the class
is a rather rare exception. [10]

The quotation above is based on an examination of many sources

which classified Negroes on the basis of color. The inference that

mulattoes enjoyed superior native endowment to dark Negroes which

runs throughout Reuter's discussion is hardly warranted and has been

soundly criticized by Goldhamer and Wirth, who put the case for the

achievement of mulattoes in its proper perspective. In criticizing

Reuter, they assert that differential achievement of the mulatto and

full-blooded Negro is gainsaid. They add, however, "There can be

no question that in these respects the mulatto has shown a decided

superiority. But here, again, this does not warrant the assumption

that such superiority is the product of superior intellectual endowment.

It is not difficult to account for the superior achievement of the mu-

latto in terms of superior opportunities."[11] And, with even more

pointed shafts, they declare:

It should be pointed out that essentially the mulatto constitutes
the upper class of Negro society; the implication of Reuter's
statement is that class differences in achievement are refer-
able to differences in native capacity, which again is scarcely
tenable in the light of most sociological research bearing on
this problem. In any case, it is not a question of whether
"real ability" is independent of opportunities which condition the
advance of others, but of whether the particular levels of
achievement in politics, education, science, literature, and
so on, which were attained by the persons investigated in
Reuter's research, are heavily conditioned by particular types
of opportunities... [12]

Regarding the assertion that since the Emancipation the advantages enjoyed by the mulatto have, essentially, disappeared and that blacks now have ostensibly the same opportunities as mulattoes for positions in the Negro world, Wirth and Goldhamer assert that Reuter is speaking mainly of formal or legal equality, which is by no means the only type of equality important in this connection. [13]

A very real question arises as to the extent to which the mulatto has continued to enjoy the advantages he possessed at the time of the Emancipation for entering positions of leadership and service in the Negro community. There is a very pronounced belief on the part of some students that the proportion of blacks in positions of prestige is increasing. The migrations to the North and the concomitant urbanization have resulted in a partial breakdown of the high valuation formerly placed on a "fair complexion." With increasing opportunities in cities for persons of dark color to secure an education, much of the prejudice toward and resistance against their entering the high level occupations and exclusive social sets have disappeared. Frazier suggests that Negro caste is losing its color basis, and that in cities the old mulatto families are breaking up and a "brown middle class" based on educational and occupational achievement is in process of emerging. [14]

This general question is considered in a recent work which takes a somewhat different approach. Arnold Rose suggests that dark-skinned Negroes have become occupationally mobile and finds a partial reason for their mobility in demographic factors. He says, "Light Negroes are becoming relatively fewer in number-- either because of passing or because a low reproduction rate is outbalancing miscegenation--so that dark Negroes have to take over some of the higher positions." [15]

In view of the fact that no reliable knowledge exists of the color composition of the Negro population today, it is difficult to determine with any measure of accuracy whether the proportion of mulattoes in any given class of occupations exceeds or falls below expectancy. The lack of such color figures today makes it difficult, also, to determine whether the proportion of persons of any given color in specific occupational classes has increased or decreased with time. The statistics on "Blacks" and "Mulattoes" in the Negro population which were collected by the Bureau of Census from 1850 to 1920, when the practice was discontinued, have been criticized as overestimating the number of "Blacks" in the total population. [16] Herskovits, by using geneological trees and anthropometric measurements, estimated that the number of full-blooded Negroes in the Negro population was 22.0 percent. [17] It is reliably believed that the percentage of dark persons in the Negro population has decreased since Emancipation as a result of the marriage of persons of dark color with those of lighter complexion.

Our data permit us to establish the color differences of our respondents and to make an evaluation as to whether the color of the group has varied with respect to this factor from one period to another. We shall give attention first to the color characteristics of the group.

Color Characteristics of Respondents. The color of our respondents was recorded on a six-point scale. The color categories are: Very Light, Light, Light Brown, Brown, Dark Brown, and Very Dark. The distribution of our respondents according to this sixfold classification is shown in Table 27.

Table 27

Percentage Distribution of Respondents According to Color,
by Professional Group

Color of Respondent	Total*	Professional Group			
		Physicians	Dentists	Lawyers	Teachers
Very light	9.1	6.7	19.6	8.3	4.4
Light	15.0	15.6	15.2	15.3	13.0
Light brown	35.2	41.1	36.9	34.7	22.8
Brown	26.9	23.3	19.6	26.4	42.4
Dark brown	12.0	13.3	6.5	11.1	16.3
Very dark	1.8	-	2.2	4.2	1.1
Total	100.0	100.0	100.0	100.0	100.0

* The total is here estimated inasmuch as teachers are significantly darker than the other groups.

For the purpose of this analysis, we may regroup the classifications shown in Table 27 into three categories to form an "obviously light" group composed of those who are very light and light; an "obviously brown" group, composed of those who are light brown and brown in color; and an "obviously dark" group, composed of those who are dark brown and very dark in color. The result of such a regrouping is shown in Table 28.

Table 28

Percentage Distribution of Respondents According to Color,
Classified into Light, Brown, and Dark, by Professional Group

Color of Respondent	Total*	Professional Group			
		Physicians	Dentists	Lawyers	Teachers
Light	24.1	22.3	34.8	23.6	17.4
Brown	62.1	64.4	56.5	61.1	65.2
Dark	13.8	13.3	8.7	15.3	17.4
Total	100.0	100.0	100.0	100.0	100.0

* Estimated.

It will be noted from the foregoing tables that the dominant color of the group is brown, with more than three-fifths of the respondents being either light brown or dark brown--the two color classes making up the category. Of significance is the fact that a larger percentage of the respondents are obviously light in color as compared with those who are obviously dark in color. (The difference between the percentages of light and dark is significant; $t = 2.9$; $P > .01$.)

If we take our dark group as synonymous with the classification of Black in the discussion of "Black" and "Mulatto" in the literature[18] and use Herskovits' estimate that 22 percent of the Negro population is full-blooded or "Black," it will be seen that our respondents show a much lower percentage of "Black" persons than may be expected from the general distribution of "Black" persons in the Negro population. Herskovits' data permit us still another comparison. He gives in addition to full-blooded Negroes the percentage of persons of various admixtures who are obviously more Negro than white. These include mixtures of Negro and white; Negro, white, and Indian; and Negro and Indian. Taken together with the percentage of full-blooded Negroes, the total percentage of those who are obviously more Negro than white is 60 percent.[19] Those comparable percentages from our data may be arrived at by dividing the brown group and taking those who are brown, dark brown, and very dark as representatives of the group which is more Negro than white. When this is done, it is found that approximately 44 percent (43.7), as compared with Herskovits' 60.0 percent, is more Negro than white.

Variations in Color by Age Groups. We may now turn our attention to an examination of the propositions relating to changes in the color distribution of those in high prestige occupations with time. This may be done by dividing our respondents into age groups as shown in Table 29. The chi-square values for this table show that there has been a considerable change in the color composition of the group. First of all, the overall table shows that considerable change in color has occurred. It will be readily seen that the very light group has decreased steadily, the light group has increased, the dark brown and very dark groups have decreased, while the light brown group has virtually the same percentage from one period to another. It appears, then, that the two extreme groups--very light, dark brown and very dark--have decreased, while the groups adjacent to them on the color continuum--light and brown--have increased. It will be noted also from the row comparisons that while there is no significant difference between rows 2 and 3, row 1 differs from both 2 and 3, with the greatest difference occurring between rows 1 and 3 (the oldest and youngest respondents).

If now we divide the group roughly in half[20] by taking those who are fifty years of age and over and comparing them with those under fifty years of age (combination of rows 1 and 2 of Table 29), the meaning of our data becomes clearer. The distribution according to this grouping is shown in Table 30.

It will now be noted that the losses in the two extreme groups are taken up by the adjacent groups in almost the exact proportions as they occur. The loss in the very light group is compensated for by the gain in the light, and the losses in the very dark and dark are nearly equal to the increase in the brown group. The significant change which is indicated by our overall test value means that there has been a constant shift over time in the color composition with a decrease in number of those classified in the two extreme color

Table 29

Percentage Distribution of Respondents According to Color,
by Age Groups

Age of Respondent	Total*	Color Group					
		Very Light	Light	Light Brown	Brown	Dark Brown	Very Dark
1. Under 35	99.9	6.1	22.4	32.7	36.7	2.0	-
2. 35-49	100.0	7.3	14.0	32.7	31.3	12.7	2.0
3. Above 50	100.1	11.9	11.9	33.7	22.8	17.8	2.0
Total	100.0	8.6	14.7	33.0	29.3	12.7	1.7

* These are "true" totals; they vary slightly from the estimates
shown in Table 27. Though teachers differ from the other groups
with respect to color, they do not differ with respect to age. The true
totals may be used in the above case, therefore.

X^2 values: Overall table - 13.92; P > .01.
Rows 2 and 3 - 4.21; P < .05 (not significant).
Rows 1 and 3 - 13.36; P > .01.
Rows 1 and 2 - 6.19; .05 < P < .02.

Table 30

Percentage Distribution of Respondents According to Color and Age
(Regrouped)

Age of Respondent	Total	Color of Respondent					
		Very Light	Light	Light Brown	Brown	Dark Brown	Very Dark
50 and over	100.1	11.9	11.9	33.7	22.8	17.8	2.0
Under 50	100.1	7.0	16.1	32.7	32.7	10.1	1.5
Difference	-	- 4.9	+ 4.2	- 1.0	+ 9.9	- 7.7	- 0.5

groups, the very light and the two darkest groups. The percentage
of those classed as light brown has remained constant for the two
periods.

We are justified in stating that the group is getting lighter only
in the sense that the decrease in the percentage of those classed as
very dark and dark brown is somewhat greater than the losses in the

very light group. The most significant fact is that light brown is the modal color of the group. One further fact of significance is that the percentage of persons who are obviously more Negro than white (brown, dark brown, and very dark) is nearly the same for the two age period categories, 44. 3 percent for the group under fifty and 42. 6 percent for the group fifty and above. This slight difference is not significant (t = 0. 28). If only the change in the two darker groups (dark brown and very dark) is considered, we find that though there has been a decline from 19. 8 percent for the former period to 11. 6 percent for the latter period, the difference in the direction of lightness is not significant (t = 1. 7). The changes noted in this analysis doubtless reflect little more than color changes which are occurring in the Negro population, and in no way can it be said that a larger percentage of dark brown and very dark persons (our full-blooded group) is entering high level occupations. Nor can it be said that there is any selective recruitment of light persons for positions in professional fields. It would appear, as noted above, that the changes represented by the data reflect color changes which are the result of intragroup marriages.

Summary

In this chapter we have considered certain factors which are related to occupational mobility. Some of the variables considered--occupation of father and parental income, for example, are interrelated, so that the full influence of each of them is not ascertained. But it has been our chief concern to determine whether the variables studied have any influence on the occupational mobility of the subjects.

It has been pointed out that the subjects in this study have occupational backgrounds in which the father, in the majority of cases, is a white collar worker. The percentage of fathers classed as white collar workers varies with the age of the respondent. A significantly larger percentage of respondents under thirty-five years of age, as compared with those fifty years of age and over, have fathers whose occupations are on the white collar level. Moreover, in each of the regions studied, the father is, in the majority of cases, a white collar worker. The proportion of fathers classed as white collar is significantly higher for respondents from the Border Area than for those from the South; respondents from the former area have the highest status origins and those from the latter the lowest. These findings suggest that though there is vertical mobility on the part of the respondents, most of them have not moved too far in the occupational scale from the level of their father's occupation.

Despite the tendency for the majority of respondents to come from families in which the father is a white collar worker, there is considerable recruitment of the present generation of professional workers from families in which the father is a blue collar worker. This fact is supported by the data on the adult male siblings of the respondents. Though there is a greater tendency for sons of professional, clerical, and semiskilled fathers to enter professional occupations than for the sample of respondents and their siblings as a whole, the propensity to enter the professions on the part of sons of clerical and professional workers is only about the same as that of semiskilled workers. A son is more likely to become a professional worker than he is to enter his father's occupation. In this respect, our findings vary from those of other studies in which the propensity of the son to enter the father's occupational class was found to be greater than that for entering any other occupational class.

It has been demonstrated also that the occupational origin has an influence on the son's educational attainment. The sons of professional, clerical, service, and semiskilled workers have educational attainments above the median for the entire sample of respondents and siblings.

Family income, obviously related to occupation, has an influence on both the educational attainment and occupational level of the sons. With each increase in income, there is an increase in the median amount of schooling received; while the proportions of respondents and siblings entering high prestige occupations increase with increases in family income.

The data have provided an opportunity for determining the color of the group and for testing the hypothesis that persons of darker color are entering high level occupations in greater numbers than formerly. The modal color of our group is light brown; the group as a whole is composed of more light than dark persons. How the group compares with the Negro population, how much darker or lighter, cannot be accurately evaluated because of the absence of data on the color composition of the Negro group as a whole. It does not appear that the professional workers among Negroes are becoming darker in color. The changes which are noted for time periods are in the direction of lightness. The fact that the group has become somewhat lighter is owing to the fact that the percentage of obviously dark persons has decreased. It is suggested by the data that the changes noted are owing to color changes in the Negro group resulting from in-group marriages and are not owing to the selection of persons of any particular color for work in the professions.

V

IMAGES AND MOTIVATIONS

Thus far we have been considering only the occupational
background of our respondents as indicated by their fathers' and
paternal grandfathers' occupations and certain factors associated
with mobility, such as those described in the last chapter. The
materials discussed thus far have lent themselves to quantitative
expression. There are, however, other factors of a subjective or
social psychological nature which must be explored if we are to
secure a fuller understanding of the problems under analysis.
Such factors as the conceptions which individuals have of occupations as a whole and of those which they desire to enter in particular, and of the influences which operate to determine their levels
of aspiration and to direct them into particular fields must be
analyzed. Such questions are discussed in this chapter. In treating these materials it is important to point out that whereas in
previous chapters we have considered the professions as a group,
it is necessary now to make some distinctions among the several
professional groups studied because of the variations presented
by them.

The Importance of the Social Structure

One is impressed immediately with the importance of the
fact that the occupational ambitions and aspirations of our subjects
grow out of the social world in which they live. This is true doubtless for all groups, for the process of selecting an occupation is a

complex of many factors, among which are the interests of the
subjects, the prestige value of the occupation, and the practical
consideration of earning a living from the occupation selected.
More often, selection of a particular occupation involves a combination of these and, perhaps, other factors, for the problem is a
very complex one.

The subjects were asked if there were occupations other
than the one they entered which were given serious consideration
as possible careers. The word serious was interpreted to mean
something beyond childish illusion or fancy; the subject was to have
given some consideration to planning for a career in the field,
to have actively entered training for it, or had actually been engaged
in the occupation. In addition, the subject was asked why he had not
entered the occupation, or if he had begun work in the occupation,
why he had changed. As may be expected, a large number of respondents had given serious consideration to making a career of
work other than the type in which they are now engaged; almost one-
half of the respondents indicated that serious consideration was given
to some other type of work. Of significance, however, is the fact
that of all of the alternate choices mentioned, only a few of them fell
on levels other than the professional. Of the occupations which were
mentioned which did not fall on the professional level, the largest
number was on the proprietor level, followed in order by those on
the skilled worker level. Three workers had hoped to become scientific farmers, one a protective service worker, and one a cook. In
all, only one-seventh of the alternate choices were not in professional fields.

There are several clusters of occupations which are prominently mentioned by our respondents as alternate choices--in fact,

primary choices--but from which the respondents felt Negroes could
not earn a decent living. These refer to certain technical occupations such as engineering, architecture, and research scientists,
in which a considerable number of respondents expressed interest,
to journalism, and the arts, especially the theatre. It is interesting
to note that physicians expressed a greater interest than any other
group in architecture, engineering, and science, lawyers a more
pronounced interest in becoming actors, and teachers a greater interest in journalism. The most emphasized reason underlying the
failure of the respondents to plan for active careers in these fields,
or to leave a field if they had begun work in it, is that they felt they
could not earn a decent living from such work. As previously mentioned the viewpoint is expressed by a physician who wished to become
a journalist, an interest which he maintained until his senior year at
a New England college. He remarks that there was nowhere, as far
as he could discern, an opportunity for a Negro in this field to earn
a decent living on a metropolitan newspaper. He adds that a Negro
employee of a metropolitan paper in New England was earning the
paltry sum of twenty dollars a week after twenty years of service.
A teacher who wished to make a career of journalism, but did not,
advanced a somewhat similar reason and added that if the Negro
wishes to work for a Negro newspaper he is confronted with the fact
that such papers are family concerns. There was little opportunity--
for one who was not a member of the family--to advance to any position of responsibility. A physicist, now a teacher, wished to enter
the field of engineering, but was dissuaded from pursuing studies in
that field when he noted that white classmates could get jobs as tech-
nicians while he could not, despite the fact that he ranked near the
top of his class and many of those getting jobs were far below him in
academic standing.

The other alternate choices mentioned by our respondents
fall mainly in fields in which Negroes are found in large numbers,
such as teaching and medicine. The reasons advanced for their not
entering these fields can be classed under a variety of headings,
not the least important of which are dissuasion by family members,
financial considerations, and fortuitous developments. These will
receive treatment at a later point in this chapter.

Our chief point is to indicate that the occupational orientations of the respondents are conditioned largely by the social structure in which the socialization of Negroes occurs. The conception
of what is possible in terms of careers is shaped chiefly by their
experiences in the community and by the advice furnished them by
persons they consider competent advisers. Under such conditions
there are certain fields which our respondents feel offer good opportunities to Negroes. There are other fields, particularly professional fields, in which, according to their view, Negroes have little
opportunity to earn a decent livelihood.

Chief Motivation for Entering Field

The respondents were asked to indicate the chief motivation
that led to the selection of the occupations in which they are now
working. Inasmuch as it was recognized that there is seldom a
single motive that operates to determine the selection of a life's
work, other motives which, in their judgment, played a part in determining the field of work were checked. Table 31 presents the
conceptions of the respondents regarding the chief influences which
operated to have them enter given fields.

It will be noted from the table that the chief influence for
the entire group is "Interest in Work," more than one-quarter of

Table 31

Percentage Distribution of Respondents According to Chief Motivation
for Entering Specified Profession, by Professional Group

Motive	All Groups	Professional Group			
		Physi-cians	Dentists	Lawyers	Teachers
Family influence	16.3	25.6	21.7	12.5	7.6
Interest in work	28.0	24.4	15.2	23.6	41.3
Prestige of profession	4.0	3.3	10.9	4.2	1.1
Opportunity for service	11.0	6.7	4.3	27.8	5.4
Influence of teacher	6.0	-	2.2	1.4	17.4
Someone other than teacher	13.0	23.3	15.2	13.9	1.1
Financial rewards	5.0	5.6	8.7	8.3	-
Best opportunity at time of beginning	8.3	2.2	-	-	25.0
Desire for independence	5.0	5.6	10.9	6.9	-
Not known	3.3	3.3	10.9	1.4	1.1
Total	99.9	100.0	100.0	100.0	100.0

all respondents giving this as their chief influence. This is followed
by family influence and by the influence of a teacher or principal or
someone working in the field. It is indicated, then, that the most
potent influence is the interest of the person in the particular type
of work, although there is a considerable amount of variation among
the several professional groups with respect to this factor. Next in
importance is the influence of some individual, either a family member or functionary in the particular field. In this connection, family
influence seems to be slightly more important. It will be noted,
also, that "Financial Influence" ranks rather low as a primary motivation, although it is clear from the data that many respondents
thought that by entering the field of their choice they could earn a
decent living. Of significance, also, is the fact that "Opportunity
for Service" falls below some of the other influences noted earlier

as a primary motivation. An examination of the groups separately reveals that there is a rather marked variation from one group to another in the extent to which these influences operate.

It will be noted that for physicians and dentists the influence exercised by family members has been primary. The lawyers have been motivated more by a consideration of "Service," while the teacher group has been more heavily influenced by an "Interest in work." Because of these variations, we shall discuss the pattern of influence for each group separately.

Physicians and Dentists

Physicians and dentists indicate that the influence of the family group or some individual member of the family is paramount in steering them into a career in the medical sciences. Next in order of importance for each of these groups, and almost of the same magnitude, are "Interest in work"and the influence of some person working in the field, another physician or dentist, for example. These rankings accord with the materials gained through interviews with members of these groups. There seems little question of the fact that a career in the medical sciences is encouraged by many parents and other family members to a greater extent than are other possible careers. The following material taken from our interview data will furnish an insight into the extent to which family members influence those entering one of the medical sciences.

One of our subjects, a physician, has a brother who is a physician and a sister who is a trained nurse. The respondent states that both he and his brother were deliberately encouraged to become physicians by their paternal grandmother, a strong and aggressive personality who dominated the entire family group. The grandmother

kept reminding the boys, especially as they reached the age to consider careers, that it was her desire to have them become physicians,
for the physician was the only person in the Negro group who "amounted to anything." There is here the implication that the physician is
the most independent person from a financial viewpoint and has the
highest status in the Negro community.

Another physician was intent upon a career as an architect
when his father, who earned a medical degree but had never practiced,
persuaded him to take a year of medicine at a college in which it was
possible to combine the last year of undergraduate work and the first
year of medical training. The wish of the father was respected, and
the respondent found that he liked the medical course and continued
his studies in this field.

The influence of the parents is not always followed, and in the
reaction of the respondents against their parents' wishes to have them
consider a career in medicine an opportunity is presented for noting
the intensity of the desire on the part of many parents to have their
offspring become physicians. One of our subjects, a teacher, took a
pre-medical course in accordance with his parents' wishes. But in
his senior year at a New England college he reacted against the program which he had been following and announced to his parents that
he wished to enter a school of business. It is the respondent's conviction that had he entered medicine it would have been only for the
money he would earn. The change of attitude on his part created a
crisis in the family, especially for the mother, who literally became
ill as a result of the son's decision.

There are other cases in which respondents have been cut off
from family support because they failed to follow the desire of the
parents or some other family member who wished to have them become

physicians. The situation is summarized by a lawyer whose father
wanted him to become a clergyman and whose mother hoped that he
would become a physician in the following terms: the oldest son of
a prominent Negro family who showed no interest in the study of
medicine had literally to revolt against the family if he wished to enter training for another career.

One is impressed with the impact registered by medical functionaries upon young persons planning careers. Here the influence
of the physician is somewhat greater than that made by the dentist.
Our respondents report a heavy impression made upon them by the
family physician and by other physicians in the community. A variety of experiences with these physicians color the attitudes of the
respondents and condition the consideration of a medical career. The
doctor is often viewed as the most successful person in the community; this is particularly true in small towns. A middle-aged physician recalls that he was greatly impressed by a white doctor in the
town who drove past his home daily in the finest carriage and team
of horses in the town. Others among the respondents point to the
rather abundant ownership of real property by physicians. Though
our respondents among the physicians and dentists do not score heavily
the remunerative aspects of the medical profession, it is clear that
the security offered by the fields of medicine and dentistry plays a
significant part in giving high prestige value to these fields. It must
be remembered that there are approximately four thousand Negro
physicians in the United States and fewer than two thousand dentists.
The small number of persons in these two fields is, in itself, a condition which contributes to the prestige they carry. It assures a
rather secure economic life for functionaries in these areas.

Another important factor which plays a part in the impression created by the physician is his personality. Many of our respondents report that they have been favorably impressed by the kindness and gentleness, the humorous qualities, and the friendly nature of the family physician. When one considers the fact that family physicians are usually called upon in times of crisis, when a member of the family is ill, and that the technique of treating patients demands that doctors remain as optimistic as possible, it follows that the doctor is conceived of as a friend and the warmth and other positive traits of his personality become accentuated. The role of the physician as a helpful and friendly person seems clearly registered.

There is always the possibility that unfavorable impressions are made by the physician who is unsuccessful. Our data offer some support of this type of reaction. One physician, though not specifically suggesting a causal relationship between his becoming a physician and his experiences with the family physician, suggests that the failure of the doctor to set a broken bone properly disturbed him greatly. The respondent has now become a specialist in orthopedic diseases. Another physician points to the suffering experienced by his mother in childbirth, an experience which has never been quite forgotten. His mother, on the basis of her suffering, encouraged him to study medicine. Today his practice is devoted mainly to the treatment of female diseases. It is clear, however, that the physician, through his personality and skill, is likely to create a favorable impression on most young persons.

It is not assumed that any of the factors mentioned above acts singly; it is our opinion that two or more of them are involved in most cases in which a respondent has been influenced to enter medical or dental school in preparation for a career in one of the medical

sciences. The influences of the parents are often combined with a
consideration of financial reward and, even more importantly, we
believe, an interest of the respondent in the type of work and an ability to grasp the subject matter. We invite attention only to the fact
that in the case of both physicians and dentists family influence is
cited as the foremost influence for the largest group among our respondents in these fields, followed in order by "Interest in work" and
"Influence of other persons in the field." These two fields have been
discussed together because of the common pattern of motivation. Inasmuch as the motivational background appears similar, the question
is raised as to whether there are other factors which may help us
differentiate between those entering the medical sciences, permitting
us to account for one person's becoming a physician and another a
dentist.

It appears from our data that physicians have a higher prestige rating in the Negro community than dentists. Among the alternate choices of occupations mentioned by the respondents, the one
most frequently mentioned as desirable was that of medical doctor.
On the total list of alternate choices--occupations to which our respondents gave serious consideration as a career but did not enter
for one reason or another--medical doctor is mentioned five times
as often as dentist. Two of the physicians took dental degrees and
practiced dentistry for a short period, but later left the profession
to return to school for training as physicians. There is no case in
which a physician left the profession to become a dentist. Moreover,
one-third of the dentists expressed an interest in medicine, but only
six percent of the physicians had given any thought to making a career of dentistry. Our interview data offer further support to the
fact that physicians are accorded greater prestige than dentists. It

would appear, then, that persons planning careers in the medical field, or many of them at least, would ordinarily have "medical doctor" as a first choice. We may then raise the question of whether there are objective differences which tend to establish the fact that, given the same pattern of motivation, there are discriminating factors which determine why one person enters dentistry and another becomes a physician.

Attention has been directed to the fact that the parents of physicians have the highest income of any professional group in our sample. The mean income for the parents of dentists, in contrast, was the lowest of any of the professional groups. The difference between the means for the parents of physicians and dentists is significant at the five percent probability level. (The median and mean parental incomes of the professional groups have been presented in Table 21.)

In addition to the fact that the parents of physicians have a significantly higher income than the parents of dentists, there is evidence that greater support of education at advanced levels is furnished by the former than by the latter as shown by Table 32. The difference between the two groups in financial support offered on the college level is not significant, but the difference between them in the support of professional training is significant at the five percent level. It would thus appear that in defining occupational goals in the medical sciences, physicians are assured of greater support than dentists at the very highest level of training which, importantly, is the most costly. This fact we regard as one of crucial importance.

There is one further fact from which we may draw an inference. The family structure of our respondents was examined from the viewpoint of whether father and mother were present in the home

Table 32

Chief Source of Financial Assistance for Meeting College and
Professional Expenses, According to Professional Group, by Percent

Source of Assistance	College				
	Total	Physicians	Dentists	Lawyers	Teachers
Parents	46.3	52.9	44.7	32.4	51.1
Other	53.7	47.1	55.3	67.6	48.9
Total	100.0	100.0	100.0	100.0	100.0
	Graduate and Professional				
Parents	24.0	48.9	26.1	9.7	9.8
Other	76.0	51.1	73.9	90.3	90.2
Total	100.0	100.0	100.0	100.0	100.0

Chi-square value for physicians and lawyers (college) = 6.506;
.05 < P < .01.
Chi-square value for physicians and dentists (graduate and professional) = 6.534: .05 < P < .01.

at a relatively early period in the respondent's life and whether both
parents were present when the respondent was about ready to enter
college. The specific ages for which data on this parental relationship were obtained were ages eight and sixteen for the respondent.
An assumption made in this connection is that it was a desirable situation if both parents were present in the home at both of the ages
specified. Either parent absent from the home at one or the other of
the periods, or both, was regarded as undesirable. The unity of the
family, as indicated by the presence of both parents in the home, was
therefore taken as an indication of strong emotional support for the
child, which has a bearing on the ability to establish some relative
certainty of reaching his occupational goal.

Our data indicate that a larger percentage of the physicians,
as compared with dentists, came from families in which both father

and mother were present in the home throughout the period of early training--up until the time the respondent was ready to go to college. Seventy-seven percent of the physicians came from families in which such a parental relationship existed, but only 63.0 percent of the dentists came from families of this type. While this difference is not statistically significant, it indicates nonetheless that if our assumption is correct, physicians enjoyed somewhat greater emotional support because of the "unity" of the family in this respect.

In seeking other factors which differentiate those who become physicians from those who become dentists, we may ask if there are differences in intelligence which also play a part in determining which of the two fields is entered. The rankings of respondents in their high school class--at the time of graduation--were compared. Our schedule asked simply if one had finished in the first, second, third, or last quarter of his high school class. High school grades are taken as a satisfactory measure of intelligence. In support of this, the following is quoted from a proposed study of America's Trained Talent:

> After the age of mandatory school attendance has been passed, the selection of students continuing in school is frequently more severe in terms of previous academic achievement than it is in terms of intelligence test score. This difference is probably due to two factors: Satisfactory grades are frequently an explicit selective factor in determining who shall continue in school; and good grades indicate interest in academic work as well as intellectual ability.

> On the basis of unpublished data... we have compared the relation between students' percentile rank in secondary school and the probability of graduating from college with the relation between intelligence test score and graduation... High school grades, in this instance, clearly predicted college graduation better than did the intelligence test scores. [1]

The rank of physicians and dentists in their high school classes is shown below. When the figures upon which the percentages are based are tested for significance, the differences are found to be significant at the one percent probability level. It seems indisputable that for this sample at least, those who become physicians demonstrate greater intellectual capacity than those who become dentists. Stated otherwise, the medical profession selects persons of greater intellectual capacity for careers as physicians and those of less demonstrated capacity for careers in dentistry.

Table 33

Academic Rank of Physicians and Dentists in Their High School Classes

Rank in Class	Total	Physicians	Dentists
First Quarter	64.2	73.5	45.0
Second Quarter	29.3	21.7	45.0
Third Quarter	6.5	4.8	10.0
Fourth Quarter	-	-	-
Total	100.0	100.0	100.0

$X^2 = 10.67$; df. = 2; P > .01.

It now seems clear that for persons desiring a career in the medical profession, significant differences exist in terms of certain background factors of a socio-economic and familial character. These differences in background factors seem most important in determining which occupational goal in the medical sciences, medical doctor or dentist, is achieved. This inference becomes stronger when we consider that the motivational pattern for persons who aspire to a career in the medical sciences is similar. Of crucial significance is the fact that the respondents who follow careers as physicians make their decisions to become medical doctors much earlier than those entering dentistry decide upon training for that field. It will be noted from Table 34 that two-thirds of the physicians made their decisions to become medical doctors before they entered college, while only about two-fifths of the dentists had decided to enter the field of dentistry prior to their college work. The observed difference in the proportions is statistically significant beyond the one percent probability level.

Table 34

Period in Which Decision to Enter Profession Was Made for Each of the Professional Groups, by Percent

Decision Period	All Groups*	Physicians	Dentists	Lawyers	Teachers
Before High School or in High School	43.0	66.7	39.1	44.4	20.7
After High School, in College, or after College	57.0	33.3	60.9	55.6	79.3
Total	100.0	100.0	100.0	100.0	100.0

* Estimated

Chi-square values and probability levels:
Physicians and dentists	$X^2 = 9.44$;	$P > .01$
Physicians and lawyers	$X^2 = 8.05$;	$P > .01$
Physicians and teachers	$X^2 = 38.24$;	$P > .01$
Lawyers and teachers	$X^2 = 10.67$;	$P > .01$
Dentists and teachers	$X^2 = 5.34$;	$P < .01$
Lawyers and dentists	$X^2 = 0.32$;	$P < .05$

If we conceive of persons having an ambition for a career in one of the medical sciences, with physician and dentist as possible occupational goals, it follows that certain factors of a socio-economic and familial character will determine which of the goals is reached. Those who eventually become physicians are able to define their goals early in the process of educational training and, because of strong support of an economic and familial character, are able to advance toward the goal rather unfalteringly. On the other hand, those persons who become dentists, lacking many of the supports present for physicians, do not make their final decision respecting a definite career until later in the educational process. This conclusion is supported by our interview data, in which it is apparent that the pattern of training for dentists is more checkered than that of physicians, and in which there is clear evidence that many respondents desiring careers as medical doctors become dentists for one of several reasons. The interruption of pre-medical training for many respondents left many of those aspiring to become physicians with the feeling that they were too old upon the resumption of training to enter medical school. Dentistry was a shorter cut to the satisfaction of the medical ambition. Some respondents who were not at all certain of being accepted by a medical school had been accepted by a dental school and entered training in that field. Others among our respondents took dentistry because the pre-dental requirements were not so high as the pre-medical requirements at the time. Summarily, one-third of the dentists thought of careers as physicians but for one reason or another became dentists. That physicians require sponsorship by members of the family and friends is recognized by the following quotation based upon a study of Italian physicians in a New England metropolitan community:

> In the case of the doctors studied it appeared that the ambitions were largely social in character. They had their genesis in social groups and were nourished by such groups which in turn provided constant redefinition and redirection of the ambition. In most cases family or friends played a significant role by envisaging the career line and reinforcing the effort of the recruit. They accomplished the latter by giving

encouragement, helping establish the appropriate routines, arranging the necessary privacy, discouraging anomalous behavior, and defining the day-to-day rewards.[2]

Lawyers

The motivational pattern of lawyers varies from that of respondents in the medical sciences. Whereas for the latter groups, physicians and dentists, family influence was primary, lawyers are motivated mainly by the consideration of "Service." An interest in social welfare seems foremost in having the respondents enter this profession. Next in order as motivational influences are "Interest in work" and the impression made by other lawyers. It will be noted that the latter two influences were mentioned prominently by physicians and dentists, so that it appears that the appeal which the nature of the work of the profession makes and the impact registered by other persons in the field of performance are somewhat common motivational factors for these three fields. It is, however, in the influence of the "Service" concept that the lawyers differ most from the other professional respondents.

One suggestive clue in support of the validity of the answers furnished by the respondents as to their primary motivation is that this group is "more Southern" in terms of regional origin than any other group. Fifty-seven percent of the lawyers in our sample were born in the South, while only forty-six percent of the respondents in the other professional groups were born and reared in that section. Our interview data suggest that numerous experiences of an untoward nature in Negro-white relations were witnessed by members of the group. The loss of property by members of the family because of inadequate legal advice and protection, the witnessing of lynchings, etc., are recalled, in addition to other experiences as workers in race relations organizations. Identification with the legal profession offered an opportunity to serve in a capacity which is greatly needed by the Negro group.

The finding with respect to the primary motivational influence of the respondents in the legal profession is in accord with the results reported for a larger group of lawyers included in Hartshorn's investigation. [3] By comparing the Negro lawyers' scores on the Strong Vocational Blank for Males with the validated test norms for white lawyers, Hartshorn was able to demonstrate that on the "Interest-Maturity" scale, a high score on which is interpreted as meaning that the subject has a great interest in social welfare, Negro lawyers had a significantly higher score than white lawyers. Inasmuch as Negro lawyers had a lower mean score than white lawyers on the "Lawyer Occupational Scale," this difference is interpreted by Hartshorn to mean that Negro lawyers thought of the profession more in terms of social welfare than in terms of those interests (Verbal Linguistic) usually associated with persons entering the legal profession. As he states it:

> ... The differences found between the Negro and white lawyers on the Lawyer Occupational Scale might be interpreted in terms of the Negro lawyers' responding to the items on the interest blank on the basis of this social service pattern, instead of on the basis of the pattern of the Verbal Linguistic group. This response would appear natural in that Negro lawyers might think of their profession more from the standpoint of a social service pattern (Group V) than a verbal linguistic pattern (Group X). [4]

One further fact which supports the expressed interest of our respondents in the social welfare aspect of the profession is furnished by the alternate occupations listed by these respondents. Lawyers expressed a greater interest in the field of social work and in the ministry than was the case for any of the other groups studied.

As a matter of fact, some of the lawyers had had previous work experience as clergymen or social workers. These fields are regarded as social welfare fields.

Conceptions of the Legal Professions. It is not surprising that a smaller percentage of the lawyers, as compared with those entering the medical profession, have "Family influence" as a primary motivation. Law has not been regarded as a desirable profession among members of the Negro group. In many instances, it is referred to as a "starvation profession." Many parents have deliberately discouraged their children from entering the field. When it is recalled that the lawyers in our sample are a predominantly Southern group and that there are few Negro lawyers in the South, it is not surprising that specific encouragement from parents is lacking. (It appears that most of our respondents who have been influenced to enter the legal profession have been stimulated by white lawyers with whom they came in contact. Many have worked around the court houses and in service capacities for white lawyers.)

Even in the Border areas and in some areas of the North a patent distrust of the Negro lawyer's ability to obtain justice in the courts has been evident. Many Negroes preferred to give their legal work to white lawyers out of the conviction that white practitioners had a better chance for a fair hearing and judgment in the courts. The conception on the part of the Negro public of the inability of the Negro lawyer to get a fair hearing for his client was supported by the practice adopted by many Negro lawyers of associating themselves with white lawyers in most of their cases and of splitting the fees. Our respondents tell us of important and well-trained Negro lawyers who refused, at one time, to take any case to court without having a white counsel as an associate.

It is not difficult, then, to understand why the Negro who has entered the legal profession has had least support of a financial sort from his family. A part of the explanation is owing to the fact that the median parental income of lawyers is lower than that of any other group. (The mean parental income is higher than that of dentists.) But even in instances where the family was able to pay the costs of training, there were refusals to do so because the respondents' parents could see no future in the practice of law. It is small wonder, then, that many lawyers have finished evening school and have had to complete their legal training while carrying a full-time job. It is only in those instances where the lawyer comes from a family in the proprietor group or in the few cases of those whose fathers are lawyers, that there is specific and manifest interest in having the respondents enter the legal profession. Lawyers must contribute more than any other group to the costs of their undergraduate education and more toward professional expenses, except for teachers who get substantially more fellowship aid at the latter level.

Changing Conception of the Legal Profession. The conception which the Negro public holds of the Negro lawyer is undergoing a change at the present time. Our talks with lawyers convince us that this is the case, for which the following reasons may be advanced.

Negro lawyers are no longer associating themselves with white counsel, even in the most important cases which they handle. Were this the case today, they would be derided by colleagues in the profession. A lawyer who resorted to the practice today would be regarded as one who was incompetent.

There is the growing feeling that Negro lawyers are not only competent, but that they are able to get a fair hearing. As one lawyer puts it, the time has passed when a judge on the lower bench is prone to penalize the Negro lawyer and show favor to the white lawyer. In the opinion of this respondent, the willingness of the Negro lawyer to take cases to the appellate courts places an unfair judge on the lower bench in the position of having his decision reversed. A judge does not like to be reversed too often. One respondent declares that he has financed cases through the appellate court in instances where his clients have been unable to bear the costs incident thereto. [5]

The fight which Negro lawyers have spearheaded for the expansion of civil rights for the Negro minority has been dramatic in character. The conception of the Negro lawyer as a champion of the group, reinforced in recent years by the dramatic successes in the Supreme Court, has done much to create a new image of the Negro's place in law. Added to this is the fact that in recent years Negroes have been appointed to judgeships in the Federal district and circuit courts, and appointed or elected as judges in various municipal courts.

Individual personalities have been of influence in changing the conception which Negroes have of Negro lawyers--their integrity, ability, and opportunities. Perhaps the single outstanding personality in this respect, in terms of the contribution which has been made to having the Negro public remold the conception it holds of the Negro's place in the legal profession, was Charles Houston. A distinguished graduate of the Harvard Law School, Houston served for a time as the Dean of the Howard University School of Law, offering encouragement to many young law graduates. His service in civil rights cases became known to the Negro public. And his record for integrity and honesty did much to convince many skeptics of the security of their legal business in the hands of a Negro. [6]

Present opportunities for playing a more active role in politics, especially in the South, are helping to fashion the new image of the place of the Negro in the legal profession. Already, with the abolition of poll taxes in many Southern states and the establishment of the right of Negroes to participate in primaries, coupled with their awakened interest in securing a more equitable place in the society, Negroes are seeking public office in larger numbers. There seems to be among Negroes, as indeed among whites, the conception that legal training provides the best background preparation for those wishing a career in politics.

Teachers

In terms of motivational pattern, teachers vary markedly from the other professional groups. Few of them, for example, have been influenced by their families to enter teaching. The percentage indicating "Family influence" as a primary motivation is lower among teachers than for any of the professional groups studied. Teachers have been heavily influenced by other teachers, and this accords with our finding for the other groups in which it is indicated that the impression made by another person in the field is highly influential. But in contrast to the other groups, teachers list "Interest in work" as the primary motivation and "Best job opportunity at the time of beginning" as next in importance. It would appear from a surface examination of the two motivations that a large percentage of the teacher group is interested in the activity of teaching and all that is involved in the academic way of life, and that others are teachers because they found an opening in the profession upon the completion of some phase of their training. Teaching for this latter group was never a primary objective; respondents think of themselves as having been "trapped."

Upon further analysis, it appears that few of our respondents are interested in teaching and the academic way of life. The profession of an interest on their part in these phenomena really means something quite different. Our respondents, through interviews, suggest that they were interested in a particular field--philosophy, mathematics, languages, etc.--and the opportunity to teach was the only avenue open to them following the completion of an advanced degree. As one mathematics teacher asserts, teaching was the only opportunity available to him. If today he had completed a doctoral degree, there would be other opportunities. But the Negro graduate of 25 years ago could expect only to get a job in some college or high school upon the completion of a graduate degree. What was true of mathematics was equally true of other fields.

It is clear, then, that teaching is not regarded as a desirable profession, although a considerable prestige is attached to it in the Negro community. Many respondents in the profession indicate that they had no intention to teach, but for one reason or another began work in the field and could not get out. About one-fourth of the teachers, for example, expressed a primary interest in becoming medical doctors; many of them began teaching with the intention of saving enough money to enter medical school. Some few became interested in teaching and gave up the medical ambition. Most of those who nurtured an ambition for medicine married and became fathers, so that it became impossible to fulfill the ambition of becoming medical doctors. It is observed, also, that teachers listed a larger number of alternate occupational choices than did the other professional groups. We are further convinced of the undesirable nature of teaching as a field of work, as judged by the respondents, by the expressed dissatisfactions on the part of persons in this field with their present employment.

Our interview data suggest that two factors entered to influence the respondents and their families to view teaching as one of the more undesirable professional fields. The first is the low pay which teachers receive, and the second is the institutional controls to which teachers are subjected. The first of the above reasons is too well known to warrant extended discussion. The latter reason we regard as deserving of more extended treatment.

Though it does not show up markedly in our statistical table, the matter of being independent and of running one's own affairs, as it were, is quite important to a large group of respondents. Some of these indicated that they would like to have become teachers, but considerations of pay and the controls imposed by administrators were important in their selection of other professional fields. One medical doctor stated that he entertained the idea of becoming a teacher, but pointed to the experience of a friend of his, a distinguished scientist who was persecuted by the president of the college in which he worked, as a factor responsible for changing his mind. This particular doctor maintains an interest in teaching and does some instruction in a medical school. In another case, a young dentist stated that his primary interest was to become a teacher; but members of his family, some of whom were teachers, did not take a kind view of this ambition. The dentist maintained an interest in teaching by accepting a post as teacher in the dental school of Howard University. The independence gained through a profession such as medicine or law is more a concern of the parents, it appears, than of the respondents themselves. It would seem that frequently parents are embittered by the controls under which they have worked in various capacities and encourage their children to seek a measure of independence through becoming self-employed professional workers, especially in medicine and dentistry. This particular attitude seems to characterize the families of our Southern respondents, although we are not able to show the extent to which this is true.

Inasmuch as teaching is regarded as an undesirable professional field both from the viewpoint of the respondents themselves and from that of their parents, we may ask whether this group differs in any significant manner from physicians with respect to background characteristics. Physicians are selected for the comparison for the reason that there is every indication that high prestige is enjoyed by this group and our teacher respondents themselves, one-fourth of them, suggest that they had given serious consideration to becoming physicians.

With regard to intelligence there is no significant difference between our teacher and physician respondents as measured by high school grades. There is also no statistical difference between the parental income of the two groups. But there is a significant difference in the amount of financial support given by the parents of the two groups at the professional level of training. Forty-nine percent of the physicians received more than one-half of the support for their professional training from their parents, while only about ten percent of the teachers received more than one-half of their professional expenses from this source. This difference is significant at the one percent probability level. There is no doubt a difference in the pattern of financing education in these two fields, with scholarships playing a more significant part in the education of teachers. It is recognized also that work toward an advanced degree by teachers may be done on a part-time basis, in summers for example, or when the respondent is not employed at a full-time job during the academic year. This factor doubtless plays a part in having teachers lean less heavily on the family for support. But further examination suggests that other factors may be equally important in accounting for the variation in family support and for the inability of many of our teacher respondents to pursue training leading to a medical degree.

Physicians and teachers receive virtually the same support from parents at the college level. Approximately 53.0 percent of the physicians received more than one-half of their college expenses from parents, while the percentage of teachers receiving such assistance was 51.0 percent. It is, then, only at the professional level that significant variation in the amount of support furnished by the parents exists. The failure to be certain of greater family financial support seems clearly a point in differentiating between those who become physicians and those who would like to enter medical training but who become teachers instead. If we look at the family structure, it is discovered that the degree of "unity" of the physicians is greater than that of the family of teachers. The difference is significant between the one and five percent probability levels. It would appear that the degree of family unity or closure is crucial and is doubtless related to the kind or amount of support received at the professional level.

Summary

In this chapter we have given attention to the conceptions which the respondents have of possible occupational aspirations and the prestige which is associated with various occupations. Very few respondents have given serious consideration to entering training for a career which is not on the professional level. The other occupations to which some consideration was given are mainly on the proprietor and skilled levels.

If the general occupational orientation is toward the professional level, the favored occupation at that level is medical doctor.
This is established by the fact that most of the persons who mentioned
occupations that they would like to have entered, but did not enter for
one reason or another, preferred to become physicians. One-third
of the dentists, one-fourth of the teachers, and one-fifth of the lawyers had given serious consideration to becoming physicians. In many
instances, to become a physician was a primary occupational goal for
these respondents. Not only is the physician the preferred occupation
of our respondents, but it is the one which most parents wish their
children to enter.

Teaching seems to be the least desirable of the professional
occupations studied. Respondents in this field indicate that they looked
upon teaching as a means to an end when they began work in the field,
but many of them were not able to get out of the profession. The field
was entered by many because it represented the best opportunity at
the time of beginning work. One important difference between teaching and the other professional fields studied is the greater amount of
independence a person enjoys in the other fields. In medicine and law
the functionary is self-employed. In teaching one is a part of an institutional set-up. This difference seems to play a part in the low prestige which teaching has when compared with other professions.

The motivational pattern which prompts respondents to enter
the fields studied varies from one field to another. Physicians and
dentists are most heavily influenced by their parents or other members of the family group; lawyers are motivated heavily by a sense
of social welfare and service; while teachers are primarily interested
in the subject matter of a particular discipline. For recruits in each
field, a heavy impression is made by functionaries in the respective

field, doctors being influenced by other doctors, lawyers by other attorneys, etc. Of particular interest is the absence of a consideration of financial reward and service (except for the lawyers). Since it is clear that a sense of economic security is represented as a possible incentive for work in some of these fields, the respondents may mean that they do not expect to derive fabulous incomes for service, but expect rather a secure living therefrom. On the other hand, there was little suggestion of the services that may be rendered through professional work, except, again, among the lawyers.[7]

There is a rather suggestive indication that the selective process which conditions the entry of respondents in one or another of the professional fields studied takes account of intelligence, family structure, income, and other factors. The clearest instance of the operation of selection based upon these factors is found in the medical field, where somewhat different characteristics exist for those who become medical doctors and those who enter careers in dentistry.

VI

THE CAREER PROFILE

A final part of the problem with which we are dealing relates to the career profile of the professional group. The career profile describes the high points in the familial, educational, and occupational background of the group studied. Here we are interested in describing the ages at which pre-professional and professional training are completed, the level of the first job, the number of different jobs which are held and the average duration of these jobs, the age at which the person began work in a professional field, and the length of time served in the present job. The number of years intervening between various types of experiences are also treated.[1] The effort here is concentrated mainly on a description of the profile for the professional group as a whole, but in several instances where one of the groups shows marked variation from the pattern of the others, it becomes necessary to direct special attention to that fact.

There are in the literature good descriptions of profiles of the type mentioned above for professional persons. Two of these are described below. Davidson and Anderson give the following profile for the male professional worker:

> The typical male professional person is one born into a well-to-do or wealthy family. He secures above-average schooling of a prolonged and specialized character with the aid of relatives or friends. He may engage in vacation or part time work for pay during this training period, but upon completion of his professional schooling he moves directly into his professional career without preliminary floundering about in the occupational world seeking to gain a foot-hold. He has three years of college on the average--few have less than that,

many have more... In the study being reported here 85 percent of professional men were married. The typical professional family had 1.6 children, a fifth had no children; a fourth three or more, and another fourth only a single child ... The average professional lives in the better, more modern residential area in the community, and a substantial number own their own home. [2]

Elsewhere the same authors have described other factors in the careers of professional persons as follows:

Predominantly, they [the professionals] come from the homes of fathers on the proprietor level, where most of the fathers were independent farmers in an era of our economy characterized as agricultural... The pattern which emerges clearly indicates that the typical professional person experiences a very limited vertical movement; rather the pronounced tendency is to be born into a family of higher circumstances, to secure prolonged schooling, and to become thereafter professionally engaged. [3]

On the basis of a sample of work histories representative of the working population of the state of Ohio, Form and Miller describe the typical pattern of the professional worker as follows:

The pattern for the modal professional person is interesting, ... such a worker's father has eleven years of formal education, was a farm owner, business proprietor, manager, or official. His son or daughter received a four-year college education. After college the first job was directly in the professional or semi-professional level. After a trial period of four years the worker enjoyed an average of 18.5 years of stable work life, holding three jobs during that time. All of these jobs were on the professional level, and all were held for three years or more. [4]

The two profiles presented above are agreed that professional workers come from families in which the father is a white collar worker and that very limited vertical mobility is experienced. The professional person is likely to complete his education and move directly into a high level job, although some of these workers have experiences at other levels before moving into one of the professions. [5] It is agreed also that once becoming engaged in a professional capacity, there is little vertical shifting.

In previous sections (Chapters IV and V) we have treated certain of the background factors of our respondents. It has been noted that the respondents come mainly from families in which the father is a white collar worker, chiefly on the professional level; that the fathers have an average of 11.3 years of formal education, and the mothers have attended school for an average of twelve years; the respondents average nineteen years of schooling and their male siblings have attended school for 14.5 years. We may now direct attention to other aspects of the experiences of the group.

Education

After the completion of a public high school, most of our respondents moved directly into college work.[6] Seventy-nine percent of them experienced no interruption in their training at this point. The remaining 21 percent experienced a break in their training ranging from one to nine years. The mean number of years elapsing between the completion of high school and entrance of college for the group which did not move directly into college work was 2.3 years. Only eighteen respondents, or six percent of the sample, did not attend college. Of the remaining two hundred and eighty-two respondents who attended college, 216, or 77.0 percent, received the bachelor's degree, and the remaining 23 percent took work which qualified them for admission to a professional schoool. Of those who failed to complete the bachelor's degree, 45.0 percent had three years of college training, 42.0 percent two years, and the remaining 13.0 percent had only a single year of work.

The respondent who took the bachelor's degree was 22.8 years of age upon its completion. There was virtually no variation for any of the professional groups with respect to this factor. Teachers and dentists were 22.7 years of age, physicians 22.8 years, and lawyers were 23.0 years of age.

There was virtually no difference in age between those who completed the bachelor's degree and those who did not take the degree but had only sufficient work to qualify them for admission to professional training. The median age for the former group, as indicated in the previous paragraph, was 22.8 years and for the latter group 22.9 years.

Fifty-four percent of the respondents went immediately into professional training following the completion of undergraduate work which qualified them for professional school. The other 46.0 percent experienced interruptions of their training programs ranging from one to twenty-three years. The influence of the latter group is such as to give an average of 2.3 years out-of-school for the entire group. Physicians experienced the least interruption at this point; the number of years out-of-school for the physician group at this point was 1.1 years. Dentists were next in order with an average of 1.9 years, followed by lawyers and teachers with 2.7 and 2.9 years, respectively.

If we exclude the group that went into graduate or professional study immediately they became qualified and compute the average number of years out-of-school at this point for those who experienced some interruption in their training programs, we find that the average for this latter group is almost five years (4.8). The separate professional groups maintain their relative positions, except that lawyers in this category experience slightly greater interruption than teachers. The averages are as follows: 3.0 for physicians,

4. 0 years for dentists, 5. 7 years for lawyers, and 5. 6 years for teachers.

The significant point to be gained from the analyses is that in both instances--the examination of the interruption for the total group and for those with interruptions only--it is discovered that those entering the medical profession, physicians and dentists, experience less interruption than lawyers and teachers. An explanation for this is not difficult. Many teachers begin work with the bachelor's degree and carry graduate programs in summer, later taking leave for full-time study. The lawyers are the most self-supporting group, and many of them carry school programs along with a full-time job. Moreover, many respondents were able to study law in some evening program, whereas such opportunities were not always available for training in the other professional fields. It is also significant to note in this general connection that the average number of years of interruption at this point in the career of physicians is less than that of dentists. This accords with our conclusion in the previous chapter that those who become physicians have background factors which permit them to select their occupational goals earlier than dentists and to move toward that goal with greater certainty.

As a result of the difference in training programs for teachers and the other professional groups studied, a more adequate representation of the age at which professional or graduate study is completed is gained if we compute an average for physicians, dentists, and lawyers as a group and one for the teachers separately. When this is done, it is discovered that the mean age at which professional study is completed by physicians, dentists, and lawyers is 28. 5 years. Physicians and dentists were almost the same age, 28. 1 and 28. 0, respectively, and lawyers were slightly older, the average age of completion of law school being 29. 2 years.

Teachers, whose average age upon completion of the bachelor's degree was 22.7 years, received the master's degree at 27.2 years, and the doctorate at 33.2 years. [7] Four-and-one-half years elapsed between the completion of the bachelor's and master's degrees, and six years between the taking of the master's and the doctorate. The interval between the bachelor's and doctorate was 10.5 years.

Occupational Experiences

In computing the average age at which professional work is begun, it is necessary to make the computions as above, with a separate average computed for the teacher group. This is necessary because some teachers begin their professional work before they have taken graduate or professional study. Unless this procedure is followed, the true relationship between the age at which one finishes formal professional study and the age at which he begins work in a professional capacity is obscured. For example, the overall average (mean) age at which the respondents finished professional study is 28.2 years; professional service is entered at the age of 28.5 years. There is a difference of only three-tenths of a year between the completion of professional study and the setting up of a practice or the assumption of duties as a teacher. When the averages are computed separately, however, it is discovered that the mean age at which physicians, dentists, and lawyers begin professional practice is 30.5 years. Teachers enter their professional service at the age of 24.9.

Lawyers enter private practice later than any other group; the mean age at which they begin practice is thirty-two (31.8). Physicians begin private practice at thirty-and-one-half years (30.4);

while dentists begin private practice at 28.5 years.[8] There are more than two years elapsing between the time of completing formal study and the entrance of professional practice for physicians (2.3 years) and lawyers (2.6 years). Dentists enter almost immediately into private practice; the difference of one-half year between the time of graduation and entrance of professional practice is owing doubtless to the necessity of taking examinations for licensure.

The respondents of the present study have had, on the average, three jobs since the time they were sixteen years of age. All of these jobs were held for a period of eight months or more and, therefore, do not include part-time work such as summer employment or various jobs which were held during the period in which the respondent was in school, except in those cases where schooling was carried along with a full-time job. Most of the respondents had some part-time employment in a service occupation, if only for a short period.

After the completion of collegiate work, not all members who later enter the professional occupations studied moved into jobs at this level. It has been indicated previously that training for some of the respondents is broken, with the respondent forced to take a job until such a time as he may enter a professional school. In seven-tenths of the cases, however, as shown by Table 35, the first job after the completion of the bachelor's degree or pre-professional training is one the professional level.

The majority of those who did not move directly into a professional occupation began their after-college work either on the clerical level or in a service job, these two categories accounting for almost one-quarter of the total number of respondents. It is clear, then, that the respondent of the present study was likely to move

Table 35

Level of First Job Following Collegiate Work, According to
Socio-Economic Level of Job and Professional Group, by Percent

Socio-Economic Level of First Job	All Groups	Professional Group			
		Physicians	Dentists	Lawyers	Teachers
Professional	69.7	86.7	69.6	30.6	83.7
Proprietor	1.7	1.1	2.2	2.8	1.1
Clerical	11.0	2.2	13.0	25.0	7.6
Skilled	2.0	1.1	4.3	2.8	1.1
Semiskilled	1.0	-	2.2	2.8	-
Protective service	0.3	-	-	-	1.1
Other service	13.0	8.9	8.6	31.9	4.3
Unskilled	1.3	-	-	4.2	1.1

None of the respondents began after-college work in domestic service
or in an agricultural occupation; hence these categories are not shown
in the table.

directly into a professional job following training, although three-tenths
of them found employment on other levels prior to moving into professional work. The table suggests that considerable variation is experienced by the different professions with regard to the level at which the
respondent begins his work. The most notable exception to the general
tendency to enter a professional occupation following college training
is furnished by the lawyers. Less than one-third of the lawyers entered
a professional occupation following collegiate work; almost one-third
of them found their first employment in a service job, and another quarter began work in a job on the clerical level.

It must not be assumed, however, that those who enter a professional occupation following their after-college work move directly
into the occupation in which they are now found. Almost one-quarter
(22.9 percent) of those who moved into a job on the professional level
entered a professional occupation other than the one which they are
now following. Lawyers were least likely to enter directly into legal

work; 59.0 percent of the lawyers who entered a professional occupation found employment in a profession other than law, mainly as
teachers. Teachers, on the other hand, showed a greater tendency
to enter the profession in which they are presently engaged; only 14.0
percent of the teachers who entered directly into a professional
occupation began work in some occupation other than teaching. Approximately one-fifth of the physicians and dentists (21.8 percent)
began their professional work in fields other than the professions in
which they are presently found.

Once the present occupation has been entered, few respondents
leave it. In other words, there is little shifting of occupation after
the respondent has had an initial period of work. Thus, after finishing the medical degree, not a single physician has left the medical
profession. Three dentists who had entered dental practice were
forced during the depression to accept clerical work, but later re-
opened their offices. Eight lawyers, or 11.0 percent of the total number in the sample, were forced to close their offices for a period after
having entered full-time practice. All of those leaving the legal profession entered work in professional or semi-professional jobs, except
for one case in which the respondent took a clerical job. Seven teachers, about 8.0 percent of the total number, left the teaching profession temporarily. Three of these had other jobs on the professional
level before moving from high school teaching posts to teaching positions on the college level; two others left college teaching for semi-
professional jobs, and two others became clerks for a short period.
In all, only six percent of the total number of respondents have had
work experiences on a level other than that of their professional occupation, once they had begun work in it. Of this group, only two percent
had experiences on other than the professional level; these "other"
experiences were all on the clerical level.

Inasmuch as the work experiences of lawyers are somewhat different from those of the other professional groups studied, a special word is directed to this group. Few lawyers are able to enter practice immediately following the completion of their legal training. Only one-eighth, or 12.0 percent of them, went into full-time practice following a successful completion of the bar examination. Almost three-fifths of them (58 percent) continued with some other type of employment following graduation from law school. Most of these were employed in clerical or service jobs. Another 21, or nearly 30 percent, opened offices shortly after completion of their training, but only on a part-time basis. These are the so-called "Sundowners," to whom reference has been made previously. Many of these worked in government jobs, drove taxi cabs, or had other employment that assured a regular salary and opened their offices during the evening hours. In all, it takes approximately three years from the time legal training is completed to the time an office is opened, even on a part-time basis. The interval elapsing between the completion of legal training and entrance of legal practice on a full-time basis is longer.

Marriage and Family Characteristics

The respondent of the present study was a married person. Ninety percent of the group were married at the time the study was conducted; only 5.0 percent were single. Of the remaining 5.0 percent, 3 percent were divorced; the others were widowed or separated. Eighteen percent of those married had been married two or more times, nearly one-quarter each of the physicians (23.3 percent) and dentists (23.8 percent) had been married more than once.

The median age at marriage was 27.5 years. Thus the respondent was likely to marry just before completing his professional training. There was little variation among the professional groups; lawyers married almost one year earlier than the average for all groups. Teachers married at 27.6 years of age, two-and-a-half years after they had begun work. This is an exception to the general tendency noted earlier, namely, to marry before the completion of professional training.

The spouse of the respondent was a college graduate. This was true for all of the groups, except in the instance of the lawyers whose spouses had an average of three years of college training. The wives of those in the teaching profession had an average of one year of training beyond the undergraduate degree. When it is remembered that the average respondent had nineteen years of formal training, these figures on the level of training of the spouses indicate a considerable amount of homogamy between the subjects and their mates with respect to the factor of educational status. It should be mentioned, also, that there is no indication that there is upward mobility through marriage, that is, that the respondent was able to move into his occupation through the help of his mate or any of her relatives. In the first instance, there was no significant difference between the occupation of the respondent's father and that of his father-in-law. Secondly, the respondent married toward the end of the period of professional training. It is likely, of course, that some help from the wife's employment may have been obtained before the setting up of a practice, during an internship or residency, or during the time one was preparing to open an office, but so far as occupational goals are concerned and the financing of the training necessary to reach that goal, these were pretty well defined and determined before the respondent married.

Like most college graduates, our respondents did not have large families. The median number of children for all respondents was 1.13, and for those who were married, 1.19. This falls far short of replacement needs.[9]

Nearly 38 percent of all respondents, as shown by Table 36, had no children. This includes 18 respondents who did not marry. When those who remained single are excluded from the computation, 33 percent of the married respondents were childless.[10] It will be observed from the table that more than one-half of the respondents had either one or two children. Only about one-tenth (10.1 percent) of the total number of respondents had three or more.

Table 36

Percentage Distribution of All Respondents According to Specified Number of Offspring, by Professional Group

Number of Offspring	All Groups	Professional Group			
		Physi-cians	Dentists	Lawyers	Teachers*
None	37.3	27.8	34.8	38.9	46.7
One	29.0	28.9	39.1	36.1	18.5
Two	23.7	28.9	19.6	18.1	25.0
Three	6.7	13.3	-	4.2	5.4
Four	1.7	-	4.3	1.4	2.2
Five	1.0	1.1	-	-	2.2
Six	0.7	-	2.2	1.4	-
Total	100.1	100.0	100.0	100.1	100.0

* Teachers appear to be the most childless group. When, however, the percentages are based only on those married, the percentage of teachers who have no children is about the same as other groups. Of the eighteen respondents who remained single--or were single at the time of the study--two-thirds of them were teachers.

The average professional person in this study came from a
family in which the father is a white collar worker, mainly on the
professional level. His paternal grandfather was an independent farmer. His father had a little more than three years of high school
education, and his mother was a secondary school graduate. The respondent averages about nineteen years of formal training.

The professional person finishes college at the age of 22.8
years and his professional training at the age of 28.5 years. During
the interval between the undergraduate degree and the completion
of professional work he marries, at about the age of 27.5. He begins
his work in the profession for which he is trained at the age of 30.5
years. He is likely to have had about three jobs during the course
of his adult working life, and shortly after completion of his professional training he is likely to begin work in the professional occupation for which he is trained. He experiences a stable work life in
the occupation, with very little shifting occurring. His present job
has been held for about twelve years. His wife is a college graduate,
and they have only one child.

In the tendency to come from families with fathers whose occupations are in the white collar group and who have superior educational backgrounds to that of their contemporaries, and in the tendency to marry rather late and have small families, begin their work
on the professional level after training, and experience a stable work
life in the profession, our respondents show a close similarity to the
professional respondents of other studies. The number of years
spent in the present job is about the same as that found by Davidson
and Anderson[11] for their professional respondents, about twelve years.

Our respondents tend to finish their undergraduate training at
about the same time as professional respondents of other studies;[12]

but professional work is entered, and doubtless training completed, somewhat later than is the case for white professionals, as gained from the comparison of our data with that of Hartshorn.[13] Hartshorn found that Negroes enter professional work later than whites; our respondents enter professional service even later than Hartshorn's respondents, as indicated previously.

Our West Indian respondents show a career pattern which varies to some degree from that which characterizes the entire group of respondents. Though the West Indian respondent is about the same age--45.6 for the total sample and 45.9 for West Indian respondents-- and though each group has had an average of three jobs during the period of adult life and has only a single child, certain other factors should be pointed out.

The West Indian received his undergraduate degree two years later than those in the entire sample; he completed his professional training about one year later; but he began his professional career at about the same time, about 30.5 years of age. Quite unlike the entire group of respondents whose fathers are heavily concentrated in professional work (the modal occupational group), the fathers of West Indians are most frequently found in some form of business enterprise, usually a small business. The West Indian is likely to marry shortly after entering professional work, in contrast to the tendency of the total group of respondents who marry just prior to completion of professional training, the respective ages being 27.5 for the entire sample and 30.8 for the West Indian respondents. It should be pointed out also that the West Indian respondents come from families in which the average number of children is greater than is the case for the entire sample, 3.5 children for the total sample and 6.6 for the West Indian group.

The break in the educational experience of the West Indian respondent is likely to come, if one is experienced, after the completion of secondary school. A considerable proportion of our West Indian respondents took jobs or entered other careers after finishing secondary school. One, for example, became a business man engaged in the marketing of pecans. Another became a farmer; two took training which led to licensure as practicing pharmacists; another was a tailor; and still another became a dental technician. It is clear from our interviews with these subjects that they did not conceive of entering training for the professional field in which they are found immediately they finished secondary school. For that small number which desired to enter a profession, the lack of finances led to the substitution of some other type of work for the professional ambition, which was considered an unattainable objective. In the case of the pecan dealer, for example, the depression following the First World War forced him to seek another type of work. There is also a rather strong suggestion in our interview data that the West Indian subject, when forced into another occupation, enters one of the professional fields largely because of the independence he associates with such work.

VII

SUMMARY AND CONCLUSIONS

In this work an attempt is made to study occupational mobility among Negro persons in four selected professional occupations which met the criteria of: (1) a sufficient number of persons working in the occupation in the community in which the study was conducted to warrant study; (2) uniformly high level training required for performance in the profession; and (3) a large proportion of males in the profession.

An underlying assumption of the work is that in studying the recruitment of persons for work in professional occupations, an insight is gained into the manner by which the Negro group has developed a differentiated middle class, inasmuch as the professions are the most representative group of occupations among this minority which can be identified with the American middle class. An attempt is made to relate the findings on occupational mobility to social stratification theory by describing the manner in which occupational mobility among the group studied both resembles and varies from the findings on professional subjects of other studies.

The specific professions selected for study were: the medical profession, represented by physicians and dentists; teaching, represented by college teachers; and the legal profession. The subjects were selected on the basis of random sampling technique, using Tippett's random numbers. The sample of three hundred persons included 90 physicians, 46 dentists, 72 lawyers, and 92 teachers. The numbers of physicians, dentists, and lawyers represent approximately one-half of the total number of males in each of these professions, while all male college teachers in the community are included in the study. In reporting the totals, the sample proportions were inflated to their universe values in the cases of those professions for which only one-half the total number of male functionaries was selected.

The study was conducted in the District of Columbia, which has a large group of professional functionaries and a long history of professional associations among Negroes. Howard University, located in this community, offers training in virtually all professional fields, thus affording an opportunity to test the relationship of accessibility to education and mobility by comparing those born and reared in the District of Columbia with those born and reared in other areas. The area contains many government agencies which give employment to Negroes in large numbers, but the occupational distribution of Negroes is not greatly different from that of Negroes in metropolitan centers of the North and the larger urban areas of the South. It is not so highly differentiated as the former, and somewhat more differentiated than the latter for the white collar occupational groups in general; but the percentage of the total labor force in professional occupations does not vary greatly from those of Negro workers in Northern and Southern metropolitan communities.

The data were collected by means of a schedule and by interviews. The average respondent was seen for a period of approximately forty mintues. Nearly all respondents were seen in their offices. Appointments were usually made by telephone and thus arranged in advance. There were few refusals and, consequently, few substitutions in the list as originally drawn. The data on occupations were classified into categories on the basis of the occupational titles used in connection with the labor force statistics of the Sixteenth Census and processed by means of hand tabulations. Among the variables studied in relation to occupational mobility were age, father's occupational level, educational level of father, region of origin, parental income, and color of respondent. An attempt was made to assess mobility over several generations by taking the paternal grandfather, father, respondent, and the adult sons of the respondent and noting the changes in occupational distribution from one generation to another. Some attention was given also to the motivations and incentives which underlay the desire for professional occupations. Finally, the major familial, occupational, and educational experiences of the respondent were developed into a career profile.

Findings

With respect to their occupational origins, the respondents come from families in which the majority of the fathers were white collar workers. The largest single concentration of fathers was identified with professional occupations. About the same percentage of the respondents have fathers in the white collar occupations--professionals, proprietors, and clerks--as is the case of a number of other studies of professional respondents which have been examined. In two respects, however, the findings differ from those of other studies. The first is that most of the respondents who come from families in which the father is a white collar worker have fathers who work in professional occupations. For the other studies with which our data can be compared, the greatest concentration of fathers is in the proprietor group. A second difference is that a larger percentage of our respondents than is the case for respondents of other studies have their origins in families in which the father is a semiskilled or service worker. In most of the comparisons, the percentage of sons in our study having such occupational origins is twice as large as those reported for other studies. It is observed that the respondents of the present study come from families in which the occupational level of their fathers was superior to that of the married Negro male workers who were their contemporaries.

When we examine the generational picture and compute the amount of occupational inheritance which has occurred during the course of three generations, we find that the paternal grandfathers of our respondents were mainly agricultural workers, independent farmers for the most part, the father a professional worker, as noted above, and the son a professional worker. If we take the male siblings of our respondents together with the respondents as representative of the sons' generation, the propensity to enter professional occupations is clearly indicated for the sons' generation; more than two-thirds of the sons, respondents and male siblings, enter professional work. Our findings indicate also that over a period of time those persons entering the professions come from increasingly higher occupational origins. This is supported by the fact that when our data are broken down by age groups and the youngest respondents compared with the oldest ones, there is a significant difference in occupational origins, the youngest respondents having fathers with a superior occupational status.

The percentage of occupational transmission was found to be lower than that reported for other studies. Despite the white collar occupational origin of many of the respondents, their fathers in professional occupations were likely to be found in somewhat different professions from those in which our respondents are found. The degree of transmission has been influenced, therefore, by horizontal mobility on the part of the respondents.

In examining the sons' generation, we find that the sons of
fathers of nearly every occupational class tend to move into occupations other than those on or adjacent to their fathers' levels in greater
number than is true for other studies. The major finding of other
studies in this connection is that sons tend to inherit their fathers'
occupation more than any other single occupation, and a majority of
the sons will be found at the fathers' specific occupational level and
on the two adjacent levels. The respondents and their siblings tend
to move farther distances from their fathers' occupational level and
the ones adjacent thereto; the greatest single concentration is found
entering the professions. In this sense, the respondents show somewhat greater vertical mobility than is the case of most studies on Native Whites; the pattern resembles more that found for second-generation
immigrants.

There is the suggestion, then, that though our respondents
have somewhat greater mobility than Native Whites, nevertheless it
shall be noted that those who reach the high level occupations have
status origins superior to that of the Negro population in general. The
occupational orientation at the higher level is somewhat different from
that of other groups studied for mobility. Negroes are oriented strongly
toward professional occupations. The percentage entering business
occupations has declined continuously when measured from grandfather,
to father, to son. The orientation of Native Whites is toward both the
professional and business occupations at the upper levels, and there
has been for this group a sizeable increase in the number entering
clerical occupations. The concentration of our respondents on the
professions resembles the occupational orientation of other minority
groups and provides an insight into the areas in the occupational structure where minorities may earn a decent living and a secure status.

It has been demonstrated that the father's occupation and income are related to the mobility of his sons. The importance of father's occupation has already been mentioned. With each increase of income for the father, there is a larger percentage of sons entering the white collar occupations. There is also a relationship between the occupation and income of the father and the amount of education received by his. sons. As father's income increases, the sons have higher average amounts of schooling; the higher the level of the father's occupation, the more education the sons will receive.

Respondents from the South have the lowest status origins; those from the Border area have the highest origins. The difference in occupational origins for those two regions is significantly different and is owing doubtless to variations in the economy of the two regions. The respondents from the District of Columbia, included in the Border area, have the highest status origins. Though some of this may be the result of the variation in economy between the District of Columbia and other regions, it is somewhat striking that, inasmuch as sons from fathers of all levels have an opportunity to attend Howard University, there is not a higher percentage of sons of low status origins entering the professions from this region. It is suggested that factors other than income and occupation are important in shaping the careers of persons entering high level, and doubtless other, occupations.

No difference was found in the occupational background level of those whose parents had moved one or more times before the respondent went to college and those whose parents remained stationary. When, however, the comparison was made between those whose parents remained in the South and those who migrated to Northern and Border areas, the occupational origins of the latter were found to be statistically different from the former.

The hypothesis that persons of dark color have been selected for work in professional occupations in recent years, as compared with the years following Emancipation, has been tested by comparing the color distribution of those born before the turn of the century with those born since the beginning of the First World War. Our findings indicate that color changes have occurred over time, with the group becoming somewhat lighter, rather than darker, in color. It is indicated, however, that the observed color changes are not owing to the recruitment of persons of any special color, but are owing rather to intra-group marriages.

The occupational goals of our respondents are defined by the social world in which they live. Most of our respondents are oriented toward professional occupations. Only one-seventh of those who gave serious thought to some occupation other than the one in which they are presently engaged considered occupations which were not on the professional level. The occupation which is most frequently mentioned by those who gave serious attention to some occupation other than the one in which they are presently at work is medical doctor. One-third of the dentists and one-quarter of the teachers report that they had given serious attention to becoming physicians.

Our respondents indicate that their primary motivation was interest in the type of work represented by the profession for which they took training. This is followed in order by the encouragement given by parents and by the impression made by other functionaries in the particular field. The respondents do not evaluate highly the service which may be rendered through work in the profession or the rewards to be gained therefrom; but it is clear from our interviews that the latter is an important consideration in the selection of a field of work and accounts for the attention given to the medical sciences as preferred occupations.

A somewhat different pattern of motivation seems to govern the selection of persons for the different professions studied. Interest in the work and the influence of other persons working in the field seem to rank high as incentives for each of the four professions studied. But physicians and dentists are more heavily influenced by their families to enter the medical sciences than are those entering the other professions. Lawyers are most heavily motivated by an interest in social welfare or service to the group, and teachers have an interest in some particular field or subject matter. Otherwise, it is indicated by the findings that teachers are in a large number of cases trapped in the teaching profession, having entered upon work in the field because it represented the best job opportunity at the time they began work. Teaching for this group was to have had an instrumental value, a step toward another career. Many of them were unable to get out of the teaching profession because they married and assumed family responsibilities.

It is clear that a great many factors play a part in determining which of the professional fields is entered. An analysis of several characteristics differentiating those who become medical doctors from those who become dentists, an analysis carried out because of the common motivational pattern for the two fields, indicates that physicians come from families with higher income and in which the father and mother are both present in the home in a larger percentage of the cases. Physicians have higher intelligence than dentists as indicated by high school grades. Because of the more favorable economic and familial background, the physicians are able to make a decision regarding the professional field they will enter earlier than is true for dentists.

The typical professional person studied comes from a family in which the father was a white collar worker and had 11.3 years of

formal training; his mother was a high school graduate. He finished
a public high school and took his undergraduate degree at approximately 23 years of age. His professional training was completed at
the age of 28. 5 years; and he entered work in the profession in which
he is now found at the age of 30. 5 years. He has worked at three
different jobs during his adult life for a period of eight months or
more, and the last regular job has been held for a period of twelve
years.

The professional worker in this study married at 27. 5 years,
one year prior to the completion of his professional training. His
wife is a college graduate. They have only one child.

The professional subject who was West Indian had a somewhat
different career profile. He finished his undergraduate degree at the
age of twenty-five, two years later than the entire group of respondents; his professional study was completed one year later than was
true for the entire group of respondents; he entered professional work,
however, at the same time as was the case of the entire group. Unlike other respondents, the West Indian married shortly after completing his professional training, rather than just prior to its completion.

The West Indian respondent came from a family in which the
father was a white collar worker; but his father was a small business
man rather than a professional worker as was typical of the entire
group. His father had two years less education than the fathers of
the other respondents. Moreover, the West Indian respondent came
from a family in which there were almost twice as many children
as was true of families for the entire group of respondents.

Limitations and Overall Evaluation

The interpretations made of the findings of this study are subject to certain limitations. First, the group of professional occupations is a rather select one and does not represent all of the professional fields in which Negroes are found.[1] Our sample does not include high school teachers, clergymen, social workers, and musicians; the results might be somewhat different were these occupations included. Secondly, the measure of mobility is made through changes in occupational level. This is a rather rough measure which needs considerable refinement. The occupational levels do not constitute a scale. Our understanding of the phenomenon of mobility would be improved if we could study changes both between occupational levels and within a given level, and in terms of some more rigorous measure of the prestige values of various occupations based upon some better understanding of the relationship of occupations to one another.[2] Thirdly, it must be remembered that this study considers only one community.

With the above limitations in mind, we may indicate that our professional subjects show greater vertical mobility than professional persons among whites, as indicated in previous studies. That the pattern found for our respondents resembles the pattern among other minorities suggests that these minority groups face certain similar situations. It is suggested that exclusion from certain fields through discrimination is one common factor. A second factor is that professional services and business operations for both our respondents and other minorites are oriented to members of their particular ethnic groups, the Jewish business group representing something of an exception to this general tendency. Since business is likely to be small business, the professions carry somewhat greater prestige.

Moreover, these minorities are encouraged to develop certain professional functionaries for service to their particular groups, often a subtle manifestation of discrimination on the part of those who supply the encouragement.

In the relatively open structure with which Negroes began their period of freedom, one might expect to find somewhat more mobility than is demonstrated by our results. That such is not the case is owing to two fundamental facts: limitation of training facilities and the fact that upward mobility to professional occupations requires more than theoretical opportunities, or even financial support. Those who "get up" must have some type of sponsorship. Many persons without sponsorship, either from family members or other persons, are able to reach high level occupations, but the probability of reaching a high level occupational objective in one of the professions increases with sponsorship.

In the sense that our subjects come from families in which their fathers are superior both in terms of occupation and education to married Negro males who were their contemporaries in the labor force, their mobility pattern resembles that found for other studies. In the fact that the respondents of the present study show somewhat greater mobility than those of other studies and inasmuch as their white collar origin is mainly in the professional group, they show some variation from the pattern of subjects in other studies of professional workers.

The limited focus of this study leaves many interesting, related questions either untouched or insufficiently explored. To develop a more rounded picture of the group and to understand in a more meaningful sense many of the suggestions of the data would require further investigations. There is, for example, a very real question of the extent to which different occupations are selective of persons of divergent personality characteristics. Investigations of this nature are being undertaken in the biological and natural sciences. They may be profitably conducted in other areas.

The relationship of social mobility to one's conception of his occupational role, his discharge of duties connected with the role, and to one's general attitudes is deserving of empirical investigation. It is enough to suggest that studies along this line will make a contribution not only to the sociology of occupations, but will be of analytic value in helping us to explain value differences among minorities and other groups.

APPENDICES

A

INSTRUMENT USED IN STUDY

A Study of Professional Careers

There is little knowledge of a reliable nature now existing about Negro persons who have been successful in professional fields. We are asking your cooperation in a study that would help us to understand the manner in which Negroes have achieved successful careers in the professions. The information furnished by you will be regarded as confidential. In fact, you are not asked to sign the questionnaire, since we are not interested in individuals. Please, therefore, attempt to answer each question as accurately as possible and as fully as the question suggests. Your cooperation is appreciated.

G. Franklin Edwards, Howard University, Washington 1, D.C.

1. Present occupation: _____
   (Name of occupation)

2. Sex: [ ] Male   [ ] Female

3. Present age (at last birthday): _____

4. Place of birth: _____
   (Place)   (County)   (State)

5. List the places in which you have lived (for a period of 6 months or more, other than your birthplace) up to the time you were 16 years of age:

a. _____ 19_____
   (Place)   (County)   (State)   (Year)
b. _____ 19_____
   (Place)   (County)   (State)   (Year)
c. _____ 19_____
   (Place)   (County)   (State)   (Year)

6. Marital status: (Please check)

   a. [ ] Single   [ ] Married   [ ] Widowed   [ ] Divorced

   b. If you are married or have been married, please answer the following:

      1) Number of times married _____
      2) Age at first marriage _____
      3) Number of children _____
      4) Age at birth of first child _____
      5) Occupations of all adult children (21 years of age and over):
        a) _____   b)_____   c)_____   d)_____

7. Health status: (Please check category which best describes your physical condition up to the time you were 25 years of age)

   [ ] Excellent   [ ] Good   [ ] Fair   [ ] Poor

8. Your skin color:

   [ ] Very dark   [ ] Dark brown   [ ] Brown

      [ ] Light brown   [ ] Light   [ ] Very light

9. Education (Please circle last school year completed):

   a. <u>1 2 3 4 5 6 7 8</u> <u>1   2   3   4</u> <u>1 2 3 4</u>   <u>1   2   3   4   5   6</u>
      Grammar school   High school College Graduate or Professional

   b. High school:

      1) Are you a graduate? [ ] Yes   [ ] No   If yes, year of graduation _____
      2) Location of high school _____ _____ _____
                        (Place)   (County)   (State)

   c. Undergraduate college:

      1) Are you a graduate? [ ] Yes   [ ] No

Please answer the following:

Name of College	Years Attended	Major Subject	Degree Received	Year Degree Received
a) _____	_____	_____	_____	19 _____
b) _____	_____	_____	_____	19 _____

d. Graduate or professional training:

1) Are you a graduate? [ ] Yes   [ ] No

Please answer the following:

Name of College	Years Attended	Major Subject	Degree Received	Year Degree Received
a) _____	_____	_____	_____	19 _____
b) _____	_____	_____	_____	19 _____

10. <u>Academic standing in last school year</u> (please check appropriate category):

a. High school: [ ] Highest Quarter   [ ] Second Quarter   [ ] Third Quarter   [ ] Lowest Quarter

b. College: [ ] First in Class   [ ] Upper Third   [ ] Middle Third   [ ] Lower Third
          [ ] With honors, but not first in class

11. Please list the most important extra-curricular activities in which you participated (Please mark X to those in which you served as a leader):

<u>High school</u>   <u>College</u>

a. _____   a. _____
b. _____   b. _____
c. _____   c. _____
d. _____   d. _____
e. _____   e. _____
f. _____   f. _____

12. Approximately what percentage of your undergraduate college and
    graduate or professional school educational expenses came from
    each of the following sources:

Source	Undergraduate College	Graduate or Professional
a. Parents or guardian	_____ %	_____ %
b. Own earnings	_____ %	_____ %
c. Scholarships and Fellowships	_____ %	_____ %
d. Other (specify source and percentage contributed)	_____ %	_____ %
	_____	_____

13. Before entering your present occupation, did you at any time
    <u>seriously consider</u> making a career of <u>some other type of work</u>?

    [ ] Yes   [ ] No

    a. If yes, please give the occupation _____

    b. Why did you not enter that occupation? _____
       _____
       _____

14. Period in which decision to enter present occupation was made:

    [ ] Before entering high school   [ ] In college

    [ ] In high school   [ ] After college

15. Reason for entering present occupation: (Please check those influences which are most appropriate and double check, XX, the
one you regard as the single most important influence)

[ ] Family influence
[ ] Interest in work
[ ] Prestige of profession
[ ] Opportunity for service
[ ] Influence of teacher or principal
[ ] Someone other than teacher or principal
[ ] Financial rewards
[ ] Best job opportunity at time of beginning
[ ] Other (please specify):_____

16. Year in which you began full-time work in present occupation: 19___

17. Number of different jobs held (for period of eight months or more)
and duration of jobs held since you were 18 years of age:

Name of job	Date(s) of job duration	Length of time job lasted, in Years Months
a. _____	19 ___ to 19 ___	___ ___
b. _____	_____	___ ___
c. _____	_____	___ ___
d. _____	_____	___ ___
e. _____	_____	___ ___
f. _____	_____	___ ___

18. Family data:

Total number of sisters and brothers:

Sisters_____   Brothers_____

19. Please check the situation which best describes the type of parental relationship which existed at ages 8 and 16:

	Age 8	Age 16
a. Living with father and mother (both present in home)	[ ]	[ ]
b. With mother, father absent	[ ]	[ ]
c. With father, mother absent	[ ]	[ ]
d. With other relative(s)	[ ]	[ ]
e. With guardian (both parents absent)	[ ]	[ ]
f. Other, please specify _____	[ ]	[ ]

20. a. If you father died before you were 21 years of age, please give your age at the time of his death _____
    b. If you mother died before you were 21 years of age, please give your age at the time of her death _____

21. Principal occupation of father at following ages: (Please give brief description of his occupation as well as his title)

    a. Age 30 _____
    _____

    b. Age 50 _____
    _____

22. Was your mother employed outside the home? [ ] Yes   [ ] No

    a. If yes, please give the name and brief description of her principal occupation at the following ages:

    1) Age 30 _____
    _____

    2) Age 50 _____
    _____

23. Education of parents: (Please circle last school year completed)

a. Father: 1 2 3 4 5 6 7 8   1   2   3   4   1 2 3 4   1 2 3 4 5
            Grammar school   High school   College   Graduate or
                                                          Professional

b. Mother: 1 2 3 4 5 6 7 8   1   2   3   4   1 2 3 4   1 2 3 4 5
            Grammar school   High school   College   Graduate or
                                                          Professional

c. Guardian: 1 2 3 4 5 6 7 8   1   2   3   4   1 2 3 4   1 2 3 4 5
            Grammar school   High school   College   Graduate or
                                                          Professional

24. Please check total family income at time you were 16 years of age:

[ ] Under $1,000   [ ] $2,000-$2,999   [ ] $5,000-$7,499
[ ] $1,000-$1,499   [ ] $3,000-$3,999   [ ] $7,500-$9,999
[ ] $1,500-$1,999   [ ] $4,000-$4,999   [ ] $10,000 or over

25. Do you have information on

a. Your father's father?   [ ] Yes   [ ] No

If yes, please give a brief description of his occupation or any other relevant facts which you may have:

_____
_____
_____
_____
_____

b. Your mother's father?   [ ] Yes   [ ] No

If yes, please give a brief description of his occupation or any other relevant facts which you may have:

_____
_____
_____
_____
_____

26. Please furnish all information requested below on each of your brothers and sisters 16 years of age or over. Mark (X) to those who are deceased. Note that in the last four columns you are asked to compare the brother or sister with yourself. (If you have no brothers or sisters 16 years of age or older, please pass on to the next question.)

Brother or sister (Specify)	Present Age	Principal occupation	Education (Last school year completed)	Marital Status (Single, Married, Widowed, Divorced)	Age at Time of marriage	Number of Children	Color (Lighter, Darker About the Same)	Sociability (More, Less, About same)	Health (Better, Worse, About the same)	Aptitude (Better, About same, Not as good)
1.										
2.										
3.										
4.										
5.										
6.										
7.										
8.										
9.										
10.										

Compare with yourself

27. <u>Information on wife or husband:</u>

    a. Age (at last birthday): _____

    b. Birthplace: _____ _____ _____
                      (Place)   (County)   (State)

    c. Usual occupation: _____

    d. Education (Please circle last school year completed):

        1 2 3 4 5 6 7 8 1 2 3 4 1 2 3 4   1 2 3 4 5
        Grammar school High school College Graduate or Professional

    e. Please give title and a brief description of the principal occu-
        pation of your father-in-law: _____
        _____
        _____

28. In this study we are trying to learn something about how people get
into different types of work or careers. How do you explain the fact
that you became a professional worker, while some of your brothers or sisters or close school friends and neighbors did not? Was
it a matter of education, family backing, ambition, "pull," intelligence, good luck, physical appearance, or what? (Please give as
complete a frank and objective statement as possible.)

B

LIST OF STATES INCLUDED IN EACH REGION AND
NUMBER OF RESPONDENTS BY STATES

North

State	Number of Respondents
Illinois	4
Rhode Island	1
Massachusetts	5
Connecticut	3
New York	8
New Jersey	5
Pennsylvania	16
Ohio	7
Total	49

Border

State	Number of Respondents
District of Columbia	72
Delaware	1
Maryland	11
Indiana	4
Missouri	3
Kansas	1
West Virginia	3
Total	95

South

State	Number of Respondents
Alabama	14
Arkansas	1
Georgia	15
Florida	3
Kentucky	3
Louisiana	5
Mississippi	11
North Carolina	20
Oklahoma	2
South Carolina	12
Tennessee	6
Texas	11
Virginia	34
Total	137

West

State	Number of Respondents
California	2
Colorado	1
New Mexico	1
Total	4

West Indies 15

All Regions

North	49
Border	95
South	137
West	4
West Indies	15
Total	300

C

TABLES 37-50, INCLUSIVE

Table 37

Percentage Distribution of Respondents According to Age and Professional Group

Age of Respondent (Years)	Total No.	Total %	Physicians No.	Physicians %	Dentists No.	Dentists %	Lawyers No.	Lawyers %	Teachers No.	Teachers %
20-24	1	0.3	-	-	-	-	-	-	1	1.1
25-29	10	3.3	2	2.2	4	8.7	2	2.8	2	2.2
30-34	38	12.7	9	10.0	6	13.0	8	11.1	15	16.3
35-39	54	18.0	15	16.7	5	10.9	19	26.4	15	16.3
40-44	51	17.0	15	16.7	4	8.7	11	15.3	21	22.8
45-49	45	15.0	14	15.6	6	13.0	13	18.0	12	13.0
50-54	50	16.7	17	18.9	9	19.6	9	12.5	15	16.3
55-59	23	7.7	7	7.8	7	15.2	3	4.2	6	6.5
60-64	16	5.3	4	4.4	3	6.5	4	5.6	5	5.4
65-69	3	1.0	2	2.2	1	2.2	-	-	-	-
70-74	7	2.3	4	4.4	1	2.2	2	2.8	-	-
75 and above	2	0.7	1	1.1	-	-	1	1.4	-	-
All ages	300	100.0	90	100.0	46	100.0	72	100.1	92	99.9
Median	44.6		46.4		43.3		43.2		43.1	
Mean	45.6		47.3		46.7		44.9		43.7	
Sigma	10.5		11.0		11.5		10.2		9.0	

Table 38

Percentage of Fathers of Respondents Attaining Each Specified Level
of Schooling and Median Years of Schooling for All Fathers
According to Professional Group

Fathers on Level Specified	All Groups	Professional Group			
		Physicians	Dentists	Lawyers	Teachers
None	10.2	16.9	17.8	7.1	2.2
Grade School					
1 to 4 years	4.8	2.2	-	4.3	10.1
5 to 6 years	6.5	6.7	6.7	8.6	4.5
7 to 8 years	19.5	22.5	13.3	18.6	20.2
High School					
1 to 3 years	5.8	6.7	6.7	4.3	5.6
4 years	12.3	10.1	22.2	10.0	11.2
College					
1 to 3 years	14.7	7.9	13.3	14.3	22.5
4 years	9.2	11.2	4.4	14.3	5.6
Professional					
1 to 2 years	8.2	7.9	11.1	5.7	9.0
3 to 4 years	7.8	7.9	4.4	8.6	9.0
5 or more	1.0	-	-	4.3	-
Total	100.0	100.0	99.9	100.1	99.9
Median School Years Completed	11.3	9	12	12	12
Number of Fathers	293	89	45	70	89

Table 39

Percentage of Mothers of Respondents Attaining Each Specified Level
of Schooling and Median Years of Schooling for all Mothers
According to Professional Group

Mothers on Level Specified	All Groups	Professional Group			
		Physicians	Dentists	Lawyers	Teachers
None	5.1	9.0	8.7	4.4	-
Grade School					
1 to 4 years	5.4	6.7	6.5	1.5	6.7
5 to 6 years	7.5	5.6	8.7	5.8	10.0
7 to 8 years	18.4	19.1	13.0	24.6	15.5
High School					
1 to 3 years	6.1	4.5	4.4	2.9	11.1
4 years	21.1	18.0	17.4	21.7	25.6
College					
1 to 3 years	26.2	25.8	30.4	27.5	23.3
4 years	8.8	9.0	10.9	10.1	6.7
Professional					
1 to 2 years	1.4	2.3	-	1.5	1.1
3 to 4 years	-	-	-	-	-
5 or more	-	-	-	-	-
Total	100.0	100.0	100.0	100.0	100.0
Median School Years Completed	12	12	12	12	12
Number of Mothers	294	89	46	69	90

Table 40

Percentage of Spouses Attaining Each Specified Level of Schooling
and Median Years of Schooling Completed by Spouses, for All
Respondents and According to Professional Group

| Spouses on Level Specified | All Groups | Professional Group | | | |
		Physicians	Dentists	Lawyers	Teachers
None	0.4	-	2.3	-	-
Grade School					
1 to 4 years	-	-	-	-	-
5 to 6 years	0.4	1.1	-	-	-
7 to 8 years	0.7	1.1	2.3	-	-
High School					
1 to 3 years	3.2	4.5	2.3	5.9	-
4 years	10.0	9.0	15.9	13.2	5.1
College					
1 to 3 years	23.7	21.3	22.7	32.4	19.2
4 years	26.2	31.5	20.4	23.5	25.6
Professional					
1 to 2 years	28.3	24.7	31.8	17.7	39.8
3 to 4 years	6.1	5.6	2.3	4.4	10.3
5 or more	1.1	1.1	-	2.9	-
Total	100.1	99.9	100.0	100.0	100.0
Median School Years Completed	16	16	16	15	17
Number of Spouses	279*	89	44	68	78

* Three respondents did not give, or did not know, the educational
level of their spouses. Eighteen respondents were single and did not
have a spouse at the time of the study.

Table 41

Percentage Distribution of Respondents Classified According to
Sources from Which Financial Assistance for Meeting College and
Professional Expenses Were Obtained

Source of Assistance*	Total	Physicians	Dentists	Lawyers	Teachers
		College			
Parents	39. 6	44. 7	42. 1	26. 5	43. 4
Own earnings	41. 3	32. 9	52. 6	58. 8	31. 5
Fellowships and scholarships	4. 2	2. 4	-	4. 4	7. 6
G. I. assistance	0. 4	-	-	1. 5	-
Parents and own earnings	10. 2	15. 3	2. 6	8. 8	9. 8
Parents and scholarships	2. 8	2. 4	2. 6	-	5. 4
Parents, own earnings, and scholarships	1. 1	2. 4	-	-	1. 1
Parents and G. I. assistance	-	-	-	-	-
Own earnings and fellowships	0. 4	-	-	-	1. 1
Own earnings and G. I. assistance	-	-	-	-	-
All Sources	100. 0	100. 1	99. 9	100. 0	99. 9

Continued on next page.

* Note at bottom of next page.

Table 41 (continued)

Source of Assistance*	Total	Physicians	Dentists	Lawyers	Teachers
		Professional			
Parents	20.0	37.8	26.1	6.9	9.8
Own earnings	50.7	34.4	65.2	79.2	36.9
Fellowships and scholarships	12.7	1.1	2.2	1.4	38.0
G.I. assistance	4.0	2.2	-	5.6	6.5
Parents and own earnings	6.0	18.9	-	-	1.1
Parents and scholarships	1.7	2.2	2.2	2.2	-
Parents, own earnings, and scholarships	0.3	-	-	1.4	-
Parents and G.I. assistance	0.3	1.1	-	-	-
Own earnings and fellowships	2.3	2.2	-	1.4	4.3
Own earnings and G.I. assistance	2.0	-	4.3	1.4	3.3
All Sources	100.0	99.9	100.0	100.1	99.9

* In combination sources where two sources are mentioned together respondent received one-half of total expenses from each source. Where three sources are mentioned together, one-third of the total expenses was supplied by each of the sources.

Table 42

Percentage Distribution of Respondents According to Age at Which
Bachelor's Degree Was Received and Median Age at Time of
Receiving Degree, by Professional Group

Age Group	Number of Respondents	Percentage of Each Specified Group				
		Total	Physicians	Dentists	Lawyers	Teachers
15-19	12	5.6	1.5	11.0	-	9.8
20-24	174	80.6	89.2	72.2	85.4	73.9
25-29	25	11.6	6.2	11.1	14.6	14.1
30-34	3	1.4	1.5	5.6	-	1.1
35-39	2	0.9	1.5	-	-	1.1
Total	216	100.1	99.9	100.0	100.0	100.0
Median Age		22.8	22.8	22.7	23.0	22.7

Table 43

Percentage Distribution of Those Not Completing the Bachelor's
Degree According to Age at Which Pre-Professional Training
Was Completed and Median Age at Time of Completion,
by Professional Group

Age Group	Number of Respondents	Percentage of Each Specified Group				
		Total	Physicians	Dentists	Lawyers	Teachers*
15-19	11	16.7	5.3	30.0	14.8	-
20-24	38	57.6	73.7	45.0	55.6	-
25-29	16	24.2	21.0	20.0	29.6	-
30-34	1	1.5	-	5.0	-	-
Total	66	100.0	100.0	100.0	100.0	-
Median age		22.9	23.2	22.2	23.3	-

* All teachers received the Bachelor's degree.

Table 44

Percentage Distribution of Respondents According to Age at Which
Professional Degree Was Received, and Average Age at Which
Degree Was Completed, by Professional Group

Age Group	Total	Physi-cians	Dentists	Lawyers	Teachers M.A.	Ph.D.
			Percentage at Each Specified Group			
15-19	-	-	-	-	1.2	-
20-24	17.3	13.3	28.3	15.3	43.5	9.6
25-29	54.3	64.4	43.4	48.6	27.1	25.0
30-34	22.6	20.0	19.6	27.8	20.0	28.8
35-39	3.4	1.1	6.5	4.2	5.9	25.0
40-44	2.4	1.1	2.2	4.2	1.2	3.8
45-49	-	-	-	-	1.2	5.8
50-54	-	-	-	-	-	1.9
All ages	100.0	99.9	100.0	100.1	100.1	99.9
Mean	28.5	28.1	28.0	29.2	27.2	33.2
Median	28.0	27.8	27.5	28.6	26.1	32.7

Table 45

Percentage Distribution of Respondents According to Age at Which
Work in Present Professional Field Was Begun and Average Age
of Beginning, by Professional Group

Age Group	Total	Physicians	Dentists	Lawyers	Teachers
		Percentage of Each Specified Group			
20-24	24.7	3.3	23.9	9.7	57.5
25-29	39.7	48.9	41.3	29.2	38.0
30-34	24.3	36.7	23.9	37.5	2.2
35-39	8.0	8.9	8.7	13.9	2.2
40-44	3.0	2.2	2.2	8.3	-
45-49	0.3	-	-	1.4	-
All ages	100.0	100.0	100.0	100.0	99.9
Median	28.2	29.8	28.2	31.5	23.0
Mean	28.2	30.4	28.5	31.8	24.9
Average		30.5			

Table 46

Number of Years Intervening Between High School and College
and Mean Number of Years Out-Of-School for the Entire Group
of Respondents and for Those with Interrupted Experiences,
by Professional Group

Number of Years Out-of-School	No. of Respond-ents	Total	Percentage of Each Specified Group			
			Physi-cians	Dentists	Lawyers	Teachers
None	216	78.8	84.3	63.2	80.0	79.5
One	30	10.9	6.0	18.4	10.8	12.5
Two	11	4.0	2.4	2.6	4.6	5.7
Three	7	2.6	3.6	7.9	1.5	-
Four	1	0.4	-	2.6	-	-
Five	4	1.5	2.4	-	-	2.3
Six	2	0.7	1.2	-	1.5	-
Seven or more	3	1.1	-	5.3	1.5	-
Total	274	100.0	99.9	100.0	99.9	100.0
Mean -- all respondents		0.5	0.4	1.1	0.5	0.4
Respondents with interruptions only		2.3	2.6	2.9	2.3	1.7

Table 47

Number of Years Intervening between Completion of Pre-Professional
Work and Beginning of Professional Training and Average Number
of Years Out-Of-School for All Respondents and for Those with
Interrupted Experiences, by Professional Group

Number of Years Out-of-School	No. of Respondents	Total	Percentage of Each Specified Group			
			Physicians	Dentists	Lawyers	Teachers
None	151	53.9	63.1	52.6	51.5	47.8
One	25	8.9	14.3	13.2	7.6	3.3
Two	24	8.6	8.3	5.3	4.5	13.0
Three	13	4.6	3.6	2.6	6.1	5.4
Four	13	4.6	2.4	7.9	4.5	5.4
Five	11	3.9	1.2	5.3	6.1	4.4
Six	4	1.4	-	-	3.0	2.2
Seven	13	4.6	3.6	5.3	4.5	5.4
Eight	8	2.9	2.4	2.6	1.5	4.4
Nine	8	2.9	1.2	5.3	4.5	2.2
Ten	1	0.4	-	-	-	1.1
More than ten	9	3.2	-	-	6.1	5.4
Total	280	99.9	100.1	100.1	99.9	100.0
Mean, all respondents		2.2	1.1	1.9	2.7	2.9
Those with interruptions		4.8	3.0	4.0	5.7	5.6

Table 48

Percentage Distribution of Respondents According to Age at Time of
(First) Marriage and Average at Time of Marriage,
by Professional Group

Age at Marriage	No. of Respond- ents	Total	Percentage of Each Specified Group			
			Physi- cians	Dentists	Lawyers	Teachers
15-19	15	5.3	2.2	6.8	13.0	1.3
20-24	61	21.6	18.0	18.2	26.1	23.7
25-29	133	47.2	55.1	47.7	34.8	48.7
30-34	56	19.9	20.2	18.2	18.8	21.2
35-39	13	4.6	2.2	9.1	5.8	3.8
40-44	2	0.7	1.1	-	-	1.3
45-49	2	0.7	1.1	-	1.5	-
All ages	282	100.0	99.9	100.0	100.0	100.0
Median		27.4	27.8	27.6	26.7	27.6
Mean		27.6	28.0	27.7	26.7	27.8

Table 49

Percentage Distribution of Respondents According to Age at Birth of
First Child and Average Age at Birth, by Professional Group

Age Group	Number of Respondents	Total	Percentage of Each Specified Group			
			Physi- cians	Dentists	Lawyers	Teachers
15-19	2	1.1	1.6	3.5	-	-
20-24	18	9.7	6.2	3.5	22.7	6.1
25-29	72	38.7	34.4	44.8	31.8	46.9
30-34	54	29.0	29.7	31.0	22.7	32.7
35-39	25	13.4	15.6	6.9	15.9	12.2
40-44	10	5.4	7.8	10.3	4.5	-
45-49	5	2.7	4.7	-	2.3	2.1
All ages	186	100.1	100.0	100.0	99.9	100.0
Median		30.1	31.3	30.0	29.3	29.8
Mean		31.0	32.2	30.8	30.2	30.5

Table 50

Percentage Distribution of Respondents According to Marital Status,
by Professional Group

Marital Status	Number of Respondents	Total	Percentage of Each Specified Group			
			Physicians	Dentists	Lawyers	Teachers
Single	18	4.7	1.1	4.3	4.2	13.0
Married	267	89.9	93.3	91.3	88.9	83.8
Widowed	5	1.8	1.1	2.2	2.8	1.1
Divorced	9	3.1	4.5	-	4.2	2.2
Separated	1	0.4	-	2.2	-	-
All classes	300	99.9	100.0	100.0	100.1	100.1

NOTES

CHAPTER I

1. The reference to the Negro middle class considers the ranking of this group on an absolute scale in which the professions are considered as middle class occupations. Some authorities, in viewing the caste-conditioning of the Negro class structure, have referred to those engaged in the professions as members of the Negro upper class. Cf. Gunnar Myrdal, An American Dilemma (New York: Harper and Brothers, 1944), I, 689-705; and E. Franklin Frazier, The Negro in the United States (New York: The Macmillan Co., 1949), pp. 292-298.

Elsewhere, in the volume mentioned above, Frazier has recognized that the Negro upper class is really a middle class group. He states: "The Negro upper class has its present status, primarily, because of its position in a segregated social world. If members of the Negro upper class were integrated into American society, their occupations and incomes would place them in the middle class..." Frazier, ibid., p. 291.

2. For a succinct statement on the social distinctions among Negroes in the Ante-Bellum period, see Wilbert Moore and Robin M. Williams, Jr., "Stratification in the Ante-Bellum South," American Sociological Review, VII (June 1942), 343-352.

3. For information on the social, economic, and political status of the free Negro population, reference is made to the following works: John Hope Franklin, The Free Negro in North Carolina, 1790-1860, (Chapel Hill: The University of North Carolina Press, 1943); John H. Russell, The Free Negro in Virginia, 1619-1865 (Baltimore: The Johns Hopkins Press, 1913); and E. Horace Fitchett, "The Free Negro in Charleston, South Carolina," (Unpublished Ph.D. dissertation, Department of Sociology, University of Chicago, 1950).

4. The Seventh Decennial Census (1850) enumerated approximately 37 percent of the free Negro population and only eight percent of the slave population as mulattoes. The other proportions of the respective populations were classified as "Black." Taken from Negro Population in the United States, 1790-1915 (Washington, D. C.: U. S. Government Printing Office, 1918), Table 25, p. 221.

200

5. Cf. Abram Harris, The Negro as Capitalist (Philadelphia: The American Academy of Political and Social Sciences, 1936), pp. 1-24.

6. Ibid., p. 55.

7. Frazier, op. cit., pp. 411-412.

8. A view similar to that expressed by the authors mentioned in the text is furnished by Joseph A. Pierce, Negro Business and Business Education (New York: Harper and Brothers, 1949). See especially Chapter I, pp. 3-30.

9. Myrdal, op. cit., I, 305-306.

10. E. Franklin Frazier, The Negro Family in the United States (Chicago: The University of Chicago Press, 1939), p. 423.

11. A recent work on the middle classes contains the following statement: "The historical origin of the middle classes lies mainly in trade, but not in trade alone. Middle-class activity was concerned from the first with the exchange of goods and services, and therefore with the use and abuse of money." Cf. Roy Lewis and Angus Maude, The English Middle Classes (New York: Alfred A. Knopf, Inc., 1950), p. 22.

12. U.S. Bureau of the Census, Seventeenth Census of the United States, 1950: "Nonwhite Population by Race," (Special Report, P-E, No. 38), Table 9, p. 37.

13. In 1940, Negroes classed as professionals numbered 114,792. Those classed as clericals numbered 97,325. U.S. Bureau of the Census, Sixteenth Census of the United States, 1940: Population. Comparative Occupation Statistics for the United States, 1870-1940 (Washington: Government Printing Office, 1943), Table 28, p. 189.

14. U.S. Bureau of the Census, Seventeenth Census of the United States, 1950: U. S. Summary, Bulletin P-C1, Table 128, pp. 276-278.

15. Federal Security Agency, U.S. Office of Higher Education, National Survey of Higher Education, 4 vols. (Washington: U. S. Government Printing Office, 1942).

16. Ibid., II, General Studies of Colleges for Negroes, pp. 56-57.

17. Charles S. Johnson, Growing Up in the Black Belt (Washington: The American Council on Education, 1941), pp. 200-201.

18. Cf. Robin M. Williams, Jr., American Society (New York: Alfred A. Knopf, Inc., 1951), pp. 84-85.

19. Cecil C. North and Paul K. Hatt, "Jobs and Occupations: A Popular Evaluation," Opinion News (September 1, 1947), pp. 4-5.

20. See Charles S. Johnson, The Negro College Graduate (Chapel Hill: The University of North Carolina Press, 1938), pp. 302 ff.; and Carter G. Woodson, The Negro Professional Man and the Community (Washington: The Association for the Study of Negro Life and History, Inc., 1934), pp. 1-17.

21. Unless otherwise indicated, the story of the increase in the number of Negroes in various professional categories follows Charles S. Johnson's The Negro College Graduate, op. cit., pp. 9 ff.

22. Henry A. Callis, "The Need and Training of Negro Physicians," The Journal of Negro Education, IV (January 1935), 33.

23. Loc. cit.

24. U.S. Bureau of the Census, Seventeenth Census of the United States, 1950: Population, I, Table 128, pp. 226, 278.

25. Loc. cit.

26. Forrester B. Washington notes that the increase in the number of Negroes in social work has been especially marked since 1929, owing to the great demand for social workers in connection with the administration of relief programs. Cf. Forrester B. Washington, "The Need and Education of Negroes in Social Work," The Journal of Negro Education, IV (January 1935), 80.

27. Ira deA. Reid, "Fifty Years of Progress in the Professions," The Pittsburgh Courier, July 1, 1950, p. 9.

28. Loc. cit.

29. Loc. cit.

30. E. Franklin Frazier, "Occupational Classes among Negroes in Cities," The American Journal of Sociology, XXXV (March 1930), 719.

CHAPTER II

1. Joseph Schneider, "Social Origin and Fame: The United States and England," American Sociological Review, 10 (February 1945), 52-60.

2. A number of studies, though not making the study of mobility of immigrants or minorities the central task of investigation, furnish data on the subject. See, for example, the following: Edward K. Strong, Jr., The Second-Generation Japanese Problem (Palo Alto: Stanford University Press, 1934); S. Joseph Fauman, "The Factors in Occupational Selection among Male Detroit Jews," (Unpublished doctoral dissertation, the University of Michigan, 1948); Beulah Ong Kwoh, "The Occupational Status of American-Born Chinese Male College Graduates," American Journal of Sociology, LIII (November 1947), 192-200; Natalie Rogoff, Recent Trends in Occupational Mobility (Glencoe, Ill.: The Free Press, 1953); and Stuart Adams, "Regional Differences in Vertical Mobility in a High-Status Occupation," American Sociological Review, 15 (April 1950), 228-235.

3. Paul K. Hatt, "Stratification in the Mass Society," American Sociological Review, 15 (April 1950), 216-222.

4. Florence Kluckhohn, "Dominant and Substitute Profiles of Cultural Orientations: Their Significance for the Analysis of Social Stratification," Social Forces, 28 (May 1950), 376-393.

5. Ibid., p. 391.

6. Otis Dudley Duncan and Jay Artis, Jr., "Some Problems of Stratification Research," Rural Sociology, 16 (March 1951), 17-29.

7. Ibid., pp. 28-29.

8. The 1940 census statistics were used because at the time the study was planned the occupational statistics of the 1950 Census were not available. It should be pointed out that an inspection of the 1950 statistics reveals that little change from the occupations selected would have been necessary had the sample been based on the 1950, rather than the 1940, statistics. The only additional category which would have been included had the 1950 statistics been employed is Architecture and Engineering, in which the number of Negroes increased measurably during the decade.

9. U.S. Bureau of the Census, Sixteenth Census of the United States, 1940: The Labor Force, III, Part 2, p. 583.

10. Ibid., Vol. III, Part 1, p. 88.

11. Karl Pearson (ed.), Tracts for Computers, Number XV, Random Sampling Numbers, arranged by L. H. C. Tippett (London: Cambridge University Press, 1927).

12. Alba M. Edwards, A Social-Economic Grouping of the Gainful Workers of the United States (Washington: Government Printing Office, 1938).

13. The comparison is made possible by use of the volume prepared by Alba M. Edwards in connection with the Sixteenth Census, which bears the title, Occupation Statistics of the United States, 1870-1940 (Washington: Government Printing Office, 1943).

14. A full discussion of the logical reasons for making such a separation is given in E. Franklin Frazier's Negro Youth at the Crossways (Washington: The American Council on Education, 1940), pp. 3-6.

15. C. H. Parrish, "Color Names and Color Notions," Journal of Negro Education, 15 (Winter 1946), 13-20.

16. Herbert H. Hartshorn, "Vocational Interest Patterns of Negro Professional Men," (Unpublished doctoral dissertation, the University of Minnesota, 1948).

17. For the characteristics discussed, the subjects of the present study resemble those reported for college graduates in W. A. Anderson's Marriages and Families of University Graduates (Ithaca, New York: Cornell University Press, 1950).

18. U.S. Bureau of the Census, Negro Population in the United States, 1790-1915 (Washington: Government Printing Office, 1918), Table 1, p. 61.

19. Ibid., Table 4, p. 90.

20. U.S. Bureau of the Census, Negroes in the United States, 1920-1932 (Washington: Government Printing Office, 1935), p. 9.

21. U.S. Bureau of the Census, Negro Population in the United States, 1790-1915, Table 19, p. 74.

22. U.S. Bureau of the Census, Seventeenth Census of the United States, 1950: Population, II, Part 9, Table 14, p. 11.

23. Ibid., Part 1, Table 86, pp. 139-140.

24. E. Franklin Frazier, The Negro in the United States (New York: The Macmillan Book Co., 1949), p. 286.

25. Based upon data from U.S. Bureau of the Census, Seventeenth Census of the United States, 1950: Population, II, Part 9, Table 20, p. 15, and Part 1, Table 44, p. 96.

26. W. Montague Cobb, Medical Care and the Plight of the Negro (New York: The National Association for the Advancement of Colored People, 1947), p. 17.

27. Taken from a handbook of the Medico-Chirurgical Society, 1950 (Privately Printed).

28. W. Montague Cobb, The First Negro Medical Society: A History of the Medico-Chirurgical Society of the District of Columbia, 1884-1939 (Washington: The Associated Publishers, 1939).

29. Fiftieth Anniversary Souvenir Program of the Robert T. Freeman Dental Society, 1950 (Privately Printed).

30. Based upon an interview with the president of the Washington Bar Association.

CHAPTER III

1. In 1910, the nearest census date to the mean year of the birth of the respondents, 56.9 percent of the Negro male workers were classed as agricultural workers. U.S. Bureau of the Census, Negro Population in the United States, 1790-1915, p. 517.

2. The comparison is not so accurate as it should be owing to certain deficiencies of the 1910 Census data. Our overall total number of married Negro male workers and the total number for each occupational category are estimates. The 1910 Census reports on male workers over 10 years of age. It has been necessary to take the percentage of

workers over 16 years of age in 1900 and apply this percentage to the number of workers over 10 years of age in each occupational category in 1910 to get the number of workers over 16. The percentage married in 1910 was then applied to the figures thus arrived at. A more accurate estimate would be obtained if it were possible to subtract from all workers over ten years of age the number who were 16 and above, and apply the percentage married in each occupational category to the number thus arrived at, for both the age at which a person enters the labor force and the percentage of persons married vary with occupational class.

3. Percy Davidson and H. Dewey Anderson, Occupational Mobility in an American Community (Palo Alto: Stanford University Press, 1937).

4. Richard Centers, "Occupational Mobility of Urban Occupational Strata," American Sociological Review, 13 (April 1948), 197-203.

5. Alba M. Edwards, A Social-Economic Grouping of Gainful Workers in the United States.

6. Rogoff makes the point that the level of father's occupation is affected by the economy of the community in which the study is conducted, and notes that it is precisely for the reason that opportunities for upward, vertical mobility is limited that many men leave small cities for larger ones. Cf. Natalie Rogoff, "Les Recherches Americaines sur la Mobilite Sociale," Population, IV (October-December, 1950), 673.

7. The population of San Jose in 1930, the nearest census date to the time of the investigation, as given by the U.S. Bureau of the Census, Fifteenth Census of the United States, 1930: Population, III, Part 1, Table 15, p. 262.

8. Doubtless the percentage for the Princeton study would have been higher had those respondents having fathers who were farmers, some of whom were doubtless farm owners and thus in the "Proprietor" group, been reported. This group was not included owing to their failure to indicate whether the father was an owner, tenant, laborer, or manager. See Centers, op. cit., Table 1, fn., p. 198.

9. All comparisons of our data with those of other studies must be interpreted with some reservation. Our professional group does not represent all of the professional occupations in which Negroes are found in the District of Columbia. The exact composition of the

professional groups of the other studies are not known. It is likely, however, that all professional occupations are represented in the survey by the National Opinion Research Center, as it represented a cross-section of the population.

10. C. C. North and Paul K. Hatt, "Jobs and Occupations: A Popular Evaluation," Opinion News, IX (September 1, 1947), 3-13.

11. It has been necessary to examine the occupational background of both the paternal and maternal grandfathers owing to the important part played by the female in Negro life. The possibility existed that the mothers' fathers represented a superior group to the fathers' fathers. A comparison of the two groups, however, reveals no significant differences. This finding is consistent with our knowledge of the Negro family. Frazier has pointed out that as the Negro family acquires property, it develops stability and the father assumes a more important role. In the group under study, it should be expected that the fathers are equally important as the mothers, if not more so, with respect to the exercise of authority and the execution of those roles, economic and social, usually associated with the head of the family. It is likely that such a group of males have family backgrounds, of which occupation is one aspect, in which the status of the ancestors through the male line compares favorably with that through the female line. Information on the subject is furnished in Frazier, The Negro in the United States, Part III, passim.

12. See, for example, the abstract of the NORC study reprinted in Logan Wilson and William L. Kolb, Sociological Analysis (New York: Harcourt, Brace and Co., 1949), p. 473.

13. Some studies employ other categories for this type of analysis. One study uses the concept "Similar" to cover occupations rated by judges as related, though not identical. These are grouped along with the indentical and unrelated in determining the amount of inheritance. Cf. Davidson and Anderson, op. cit., p. 30, passim. At least one other study has used the general status of the father together with the two adjacent statuses in determining the amount of transmission. Cf. Centers, op. cit., p. 200.

14. Davidson and Anderson, op. cit., Table 7, p. 31.

15. Pitirim Sorokin, Social Mobility (New York: Harper and Brothers, 1927), Table 1, p. 422; and Table 2, p. 423.

16. Sorokin, op. cit., p. 124.

17. On the basis of a study of the occupations of 2,314 Negro college graduates up to 1899, DuBois found that 53.4 percent of them became clergymen and 16.8 percent were teachers. Thus, approximately 70 percent of the graduates included in the study were in these two professions. Cf. W. E. B. DuBois, "The Talented Tenth,", in W. E. B. DuBois and Booker T. Washington (eds.), The Negro Problem (New York: James Pott and Co., 1903), p. 52.

CHAPTER IV

1. Our respondents from this region are mainly from the District of Columbia. Other cities of the region from which they come are: Baltimore, Maryland; Wilmington, Delaware; Indianapolis, Indiana; St. Louis, Missouri; and Kansas City, Kansas.

2. This assumption applies more to Southern respondents than to those from the North. In many Northern communities the opportunity to secure a professional education at home is available.

3. This interpretation has been checked with West Indian students and with a social scientist who has traveled in the West Indies and conducted research in race relations in that area. Both students and the social scientist are in agreement with the viewpoint expressed in the text.

4. The general belief is that migrants tend to become occupationally mobile. For a number of interesting tests of the relationship between migration and occupational mobility, see Ronald Freedman and Amos Hawley, "Migration and Occupational Mobility in the Depression," American Journal of Sociology, LV (September 1949), 170-177.

5. This step reduces the error created by the bias of selection, but it does not eliminate it. The parents represent a superior group. Doubtless many of the factors operating to get the respondent into a high level occupation have influenced the siblings as well.

6. That the factors of occupation and income are important in determining how far one goes in the educational world has been amply demonstrated in previous studies. See, for example, the following:

Howard Bell, Youth Tell Their Story (Washington: American Council
on Education, 1938), Table 16, p. 61; and Elbridge Sibley, "Some
Demographic Clues to Stratification," American Sociological Review,
7 (June 1942), 326ff. Both of the above works conclude that there is
a positive relationship between father's occupational status and the
educational attainment of his sons.   With regard to this relationship, Sibley elsewhere states, "A boy or girl who graduated from
high school in New York State in 1940--the last year before the war--
was more than two and a half times as likely to go to college if his
parents' income exceeded $9,000 as if it was less than $5,000..."
Cf. Elbridge Sibley, "The Relation between College Attendance and
Economic Status," Report of the Temporary Commission on the Need
for a State University (Albany, New York: Williams Press, Inc.,
1948), p. 113.

7. The inference may be made that this figure is high by taking more
recent figures on the income of Nonwhite families. With the inflated
wages and salaries of the present period, the median income of Nonwhite families in 1952 was only $2,338. Cf. Bureau of the Census,
"Family Income in the United States: 1952," Current Population Reports, Series P-60, No. 15, April 27, 1954, Table 6, p. 11.

8. Figures on the last school year completed were not taken by the
Census Bureau until 1940. Prior to that time, figures for those attending school and the percentage illiterate were given. As the educational
level of the Negro population has continued to rise, it is fair to compare our medians with those from the 1950 Census. In 1950, the median amount of schooling completed by Negro males and females 25
years of age and over were 6.9 and 7.7 years, respectively. Cf. U.S.
Bureau of the Census, Seventeenth Census of the United States, 1950:
"Nonwhite Population by Race," (Washington: Government Printing Office, 1953), Table 9, p. 27.

9. William H. Form and Delbert C. Miller, "Occupational Career
Pattern as a Sociological Instrument," American Journal of Sociology,
LIV (January 1949), 327.

10. Edward B. Reuter, The Mulatto in the United States (Boston: The
Gorham Press, 1918), pp. 379-380.

11. Louis Wirth and Herbert Goldhamer, "The Hybrid and the Problem
of Miscegenation," in Otto Klineberg (ed.), Characteristics of the American Negro (New York: Harper and Brothers, 1944), Part V, p. 335.

12. Wirth and Goldhamer, p. 356.

13. Loc. cit.

14. E. Franklin Frazier, The Negro Family in the United States, pp. 398, 399, 429, passim.

15. Arnold M. Rose, The Negro's Morale, (Minneapolis: The University of Minnesota Press, 1949), pp. 63-64.

16. Melville J. Herskovits, The Antropometry of the American Negro, (New York: Columbia University Press, 1930), p. 18.

17. Ibid., p. 15.

18. The terms "Black" and "Mulatto" have been used somewhat loosely in the literature. Persons showing any admixture of Negro and white blood were sometimes classified as "Mulatto."

19. Herskovits, op. cit., p. 15.

20. To divide the group equally in half, according to age, we would have to take those fifty-one years of age and over and compare them with those under that age. The age range of the respondents is from 22 to 80 years of age.

CHAPTER V

1. Dael Wolfle, "Plans for Studies of America's Trained Talent," Items (New York: The Social Science Research Council), Vol. 5, No. 1, (March 1951), p. 4.

2. Oswald Hall, "The Stages of a Medical Career," American Journal of Sociology, LIII (March 1948), 328.

3. Herbert H. Hartshorn, "Vocational Interest Patterns of Negro Professional Men," op. cit.

4. Ibid., p. 42-43. In this connection, it appears that Negro professional persons have greater welfare interests than white professionals in general. "The higher social service scores of the Negro groups are

compatible with their higher interest-maturity. The tendency for the
Negro groups to rate high in the social service areas and to mark in
the direction of more liberal attitudes, values and beliefs, might be
the main reason why they rate high on the interest-maturity scale and
fail to rate higher on the respective professional scales. White lawyers, life insurance salesmen, and physicians rate less high on the
social service scales."

5. As Negroes become more active in politics, it is less likely that
they will be dealt with differentially in the courts. A study of a Southern community points out that where white judges are elected and Negroes
vote, a judge is prone to consider the Negro lawyer in much the same
manner as he does other lawyers, owing to the former's political influence in the Negro community. Cf. Harry J. Walker, "A Study of Race
Accommodation in a Southern Community," (Unpublished doctoral dissertation, The University of Chicago, 1945).

6. There are today Negro lawyers who are better known to the Negro
masses than was Charles Houston. Thurgood Marshall, who heads the
legal staff of the National Association for the Advancement of Colored
People, is well known through his role of chief advocate in most of the
recent civil rights cases in which the Association has participated and
has become something of a popular hero. Marshall was selected for
work with the Association by Houston, who started the NAACP's work
in the area of civil rights. Judge William H. Hastie of the United
States Third Circuit Court of Appeals is also well known among the
Negro masses. Hastie's previous experiences as Civilian Adviser to
the Secretary of War and as Governor of the Virgin Isles brought him
to the attention of the public before his appointment to the bench. It is
enough to remark in passing that the rise of Negroes to important legal
and judicial positions continues apace. Judge Harold Stevens, a former
municipal judge in New York City, has recently been appointed to the
Supreme Court of the State of New York. George W. Crawford, a distinguished Yale Law graduate and esteemed member of the New Haven
Bar, is now serving as the Corporation Counsel of the City of New
Haven, Connecticut.

7. The motivational patterns operating within business and professional
structures do not vary as much as the ideal typical conceptualization of
these patterns suggest. The business man is concerned with prestige
considerations as well as with "profits," while the professional functionary is concerned with economic rewards as well as with the rendi-
tion of service and the esteem associated with the demonstrations of

his skills. For an interesting discussion of this point, see Talcott Parsons, "The Professions and Social Structure," Social Forces, XVII (May 1939), 457-467.

CHAPTER VI

1. Most of the tables supporting the conclusions drawn in this chapter are found in Appendix "C".

2. Dewey Anderson and Percy E. Davidson, Ballots and the Democratic Class Struggle (Palo Alto: Stanford University Press, 1943), pp. 83-84.

3. Percy E. Davidson and H. Dewey Anderson, Occupational Mobility in an American Community (Palo Alto: Stanford University Press, 1937), p. 105.

4. William H. Form and Delbert C. Miller, "Occupational Career Pattern as a Sociological Instrument," American Journal of Sociology, LIV (January 1949), 327-328.

5. In the study of the San Jose community, the authors found that 41 percent of the professional subjects began their work careers on the professional level. Cf. Percy E. Davidson and H. Dewey Anderson, Occupational Mobility in an American Community, p. 98.

6. The analysis is based on 274 cases. Eighteen respondents did not attend college; four of them did not attend high school but were taught by tutors or family members in preparation for advanced training; and four others took college work after having completed professional training.

7. The teachers had varying amounts of training. Three had the bachelor's degree as the highest earned degree, while the Master's degree was the highest degree held by 37 others. Of the 52 teachers holding the doctorate, four did not take the Master's degree, moving directly from the bachelor's to the doctorate.

8. The mean age at which the physician respondents of this study began private practice is two years later than the comparable age of those studied by Hartshorn. Two factors doubtless influence this result:

(1) our physician respondents average approximately a half year more of formal training; and (2) there is doubtless a larger proportion of the present sample who are specialists as the Washington metropolitan community has the largest number of Negro specialists of any area in the country. Specialists spend more time in hospitals before beginning private practice. The lawyer group in our sample began practice later than the group studied by Hartshorn; the difference is about two years. Doubtless the ability to continue in a job in the Federal Government after graduation from law school played a part in this result. (The mean ages at the time of beginning practice for Hartshorn's group are given in H. H. Hartshorn, op. cit., pp. 23, 33.)

9. It is estimated that married college graduates should have at least 2.1 children if they are to replace themselves in the next generation. Cf. Clarence J. Gamble, "The College Birthrate," Journal of Heredity, XXXVIII (December 1947), 355.

10. It is to be remembered that the wives of all of these respondents are not yet through their child-bearing period. It is reasonable to assume, however, that no great alteration of the figures reported will be experienced after all of the wives have passed through their period of fecundity. The first child is born two and a half years after the respondent marries, or about the time the respondent is thirty years of age. There are sixteen years between the age of the respondent when the first child was born and the median age at the time this study was conducted. It is believed that during those sixteen years, most of those who were to have other children have had them and thus have completed their families.

11. Davidson and Anderson, Occupational Mobility in an American Community, op. cit., Table 92, p. 177.

12. The median age at which our teacher group finishes the undergraduate degree is almost the same as the mean age reported in a survey of 4,667 members of the American Association of University Professors. Our average was 22.7 years; that reported for members of the Association was 23.2 years. Cf. B. W. Kunkel, "A Survey of College Faculties," Bulletin of the Association of American Colleges, XXIII, (March 1937), 255.

13. H. H. Hartshorn, op. cit., pp. 27, 33, passim.

CHAPTER VII

1.   These occupations are among those which have the highest prestige values in the nation as a whole.   See Davidson and Anderson, <u>Ballots and the Democratic Class Struggle</u>, p. 98.

2.   Paul Hatt has invited attention to this fact in his discussion of occupational situses.   See Paul K. Hatt, "Occupation and Social Stratification," <u>American Journal of Sociology</u>, LV (May 1950), 542.

BIBLIOGRAPHY

Adams, Stuart. "Regional Differences in Vertical Mobility in a High-Status Occupation," American Sociological Review, XV (April 1950), 228-235.

Anderson, Dewey, and Davidson, Percy E. Ballots and the Democratic Class Struggle. Palo Alto: Stanford University Press, 1937.

Anderson, W. A. Marriages and Families of University Graduates. Ithaca, New York: Cornell University Press, 1950.

Bell, Howard. Youth Tell Their Story. Washington: American Council on Education, 1938.

Callis, Henry A. "The Need and Training of Negro Physicians," The Journal of Negro Education, IV (January 1935), 32-41.

Centers, Richard. "Occupational Mobility of Urban Occupational Strata," American Sociological Review, XIII (April 1948), 197-203.

Cobb, W. Montague. Medical Care and the Plight of the Negro. New York: The National Association for the Advancement of Colored People, 1947.

——. The First Negro Medical Society: A History of the Medico-Chirurgical Society of the District of Columbia, 1884-1939. Washington: The Associated Publishers, 1939.

Davidson, Percy, and Anderson, H. Dewey. Occupational Mobility in an American Community. Palo Alto: Stanford University Press, 1937.

DuBois, W. E. B. "The Talented Tenth," in The Negro Problem. Edited by W. E. B. DuBois and Booker T. Washington. New York: James Pott and Co., 1903.

Duncan, Otis Dudley, and Artis, Jay, Jr. "Some Problems of Stratification Research," Rural Sociology, XVI (March 1951), 17-29.

Edwards, Alba M. A Social-Economic Grouping of the Gainful Workers of the United States, 1870-1940. Washington: Government Printing Office, 1943.

Fauman, S. Joseph. "The Factors in Occupational Selection among Male Detroit Jews," Unpublished doctoral dissertation, Department of Sociology, University of Michigan, 1948.

216

Federal Security Agency, U.S. Office of Education. General Studies of Colleges for Negroes, Vol. II.

——. National Survey of Higher Education, 4 Vols. Washington: Government Printing Office, 1942.

Fiftieth Anniversary Souvenir Program of the Robert T. Freeman Dental Society, 1950. (Privately Printed.)

Fitchett, E. Horace. "The Free Negro in Charleston, South Carolina," Unpublished doctoral dissertation, Department of Sociology, University of Chicago, 1950.

Form, William H. and Miller, Delbert C. "Occupational Career Pattern as a Sociological Instrument," American Journal of Sociology, LIV (January 1949), 317-329.

Franklin, John Hope. The Free Negro in North Carolina, 1790-1860. Chapel Hill: University of North Carolina Press, 1943.

Frazier, E. Franklin. The Negro in the United States. New York: The Macmillan Co., 1949.

——. The Negro Family in the United States. Chicago: University of Chicago Press, 1939.

——. Negro Youth at the Crossways. Washington: American Council on Education, 1940.

——. "Occupational Classes among Negroes in Cities," American Journal of Sociology, XXXV (March 1930), 718-738.

Freedman, Ronald, and Hawley, Amos. "Migration and Occupational Mobility in the Depression," American Journal of Sociology, LV (September 1949), 170-177.

Gamble, Clarence. "The College Birthrate," Journal of Heredity, XXXVIII (December 1947), 355-362.

Hall, Oswald. "The Stages of a Medical Career," American Journal of Sociology, LIII (March 1948), 327-336.

Handbook of the Medico-Chirurgical Society, 1950. (Privately printed.)

Harris, Abram L. The Negro as Capitalist. Philadelphia: The American Academy of Political and Social Sciences, 1936.

Hartshorn, Herbert H. "Vocational Interest Patterns of Negro Professional Men," Unpublished doctoral dissertation, University of Minnesota, 1948.

Hatt, Paul K. "Occupation and Social Stratification," American Journal of Sociology, LV (May 1950), 533-543.

——. "Stratification in the Mass Society," American Sociological Review, XV (April 1950), 216-222.

Herskovits, Melville J. The Anthropometry of the American Negro. New York: Columbia University Press, 1930.

Johnson, Charles S. Growing Up in the Black Belt. Washington: American Council on Education, 1941.

——. The Negro College Graduate. Chapel Hill: University of North Carolina Press, 1938.

Kluckhohn, Florence. "Dominant and Substitute Profiles of Cultural Orientation: Their Significance for the Analysis of Social Stratification," Social Forces, XXVIII (May 1950), 376-393.

Kunkel, B. W. "A Survey of College Faculties," Bulletin of the Association of American Colleges, XXIII (March 1937), 463-514.

Kwoh, Beulah Ong. "The Occupational Status of American-Born Chinese Male College Graduates," American Journal of Sociology, LIII (November 1947), 192-200.

Lewis, Roy, and Maude, Angus. The English Middle Classes. New York: Alfred A. Knopf, Inc., 1950.

Moore, Wilbert, and Williams, Robin M., Jr. "Stratification in the Ante-Bellum South," American Sociological Review, VII (June 1942), 343-352.

Myrdal, Gunnar. An American Dilemma. New York: Harper and Brothers, 1944.

North, C. C., and Hatt, Paul K. "Jobs and Occupations: A Popular Evaluation," Opinion News, IX (September 1, 1947), 3-13.

Parrish, C. H. "Color Names and Color Notions," Journal of Negro Education, (Winter 1946), 13-20.

Parsons, Talcott. "The Professions and Social Structure," Social Forces (May 1939), 457-467.

Reid, Ira deA. "Fifty Years of Progress in the Professions," The Pittsburgh Courier, July 1, 1950, 8-9.

Rogoff, Natalie. "Les Recherches Americaines Sur la Mobilite Sociale," Population, IV (October-December 1950), 669-688.

Rogoff, Natalie. Recent Trends in Occupational Mobility. Glencoe, Ill.: The Free Press, 1953.

Rose, Arnold. The Negro's Morale. Minneapolis: University of Minnesota Press, 1949.

Russell, John H. The Free Negro in Virginia, 1619-1865. Baltimore: The Johns Hopkins Press, 1913.

Schneider, Joseph. "Social Origin and Fame: The United States and England," American Sociological Review, X (February 1945), 52-60.

Sibley, Elbridge. "Some Demographic Clues to Stratification," American Sociological Review, VII (June 1942), 322-330.

——. "The Relation between College Attendance and Economic Status," in Report of the Temporary Commission on the Need for a State University. Albany, New York: Williams Press, Inc., 1948, pp. 113-126.

Sorokin, Pitirim. Social Mobility. New York: Harper and Brothers, 1927.

Strong, Edward K., Jr. The Second-Generation Japanese Problem. Palo Alto: Stanford University Press, 1934.

Tippett, L. H. C. "Random Sampling Numbers," in Tracts for Computers. Edited by Karl Pearson. London: Cambridge University Press, 1927.

U.S. Bureau of the Census. Fifteenth Census of the United States, 1930: Population, III, Washington: Government Printing Office, 1932.

——. "Family Income in the United States: 1952," Current Population Reports, Series P-60, No. 15. Washington: Government Printing Office, April 27, 1954.

——. Negro Population in the United States, 1790-1915. Washington: Government Printing Office, 1918.

——. Negroes in the United States, 1920-1932. Washington: Government Printing Office, 1935.

——. Sixteenth Census of the United States, 1940: Comparative Occupation Statistics for the United States, 1870-1940. Washington: Government Printing Office, 1943.

——. Sixteenth Census of the United States, 1940: The Labor Force, III. Washington: Government Printing Office, 1943.

U.S. Bureau of the Census. Seventeenth Census of the United States, 1950: Population, I. Washington: Government Printing Office, 1953.

——. Seventeenth Census of the United States, 1950: Population, II. Washington: Government Printing Office, 1953.

——. Seventeenth Census of the United States, 1950: "Nonwhite Population by Race," Special Report, P-E, No. 38. Washington: Government Printing Office, 1953.

——. Seventeenth Census of the United States, 1950: U. S. Summary, Bulletin P-C1. Washington: Government Printing Office, 1953.

Walker, Harry J. "A Study of Race Accommodation in a Southern Community," Unpublished doctoral dissertation, Department of Sociology, University of Chicago, 1945.

Washington, Forrester B. "The Need and Education of Negroes in Social Work," The Journal of Negro Education, IV (January 1935), 76-93.

Williams, Robin M., Jr. American Society. New York: Alfred A. Knopf, Inc., 1951.

Wilson, Logan, and Kolb, William. Sociological Analysis. New York: Harcourt, Brace and Co., 1949.

Wirth, Louis, and Goldhamer, Herbert. "The Hybrid and the Problem of Miscegenation," in Characteristics of the American Negro. Edited by Otto Klinebert. New York: Harper and Brothers, 1944.

Wolfe, Dael. "Plans for Studies of America's Trained Talent," Items, 5 (March 1951). New York: Social Science Research Council.

Woodson, Carter G. The Negro Professional Man and the Community. Washington: The Association for the Study of Negro Life and History, Inc., 1934.

INDEX

Age
mobility by, 77-79.
father's education and, 102-105.
at high points in career, 169.

Anderson, H. Dewey, 57-59, 70, 205.

Artis, Jay, Jr., 30.

Business, Negro, 19.
attitude of businessmen toward education of sons, 93.

Census
use in classifying occupations, 37-38.
statistics on color, 108, 199.

Centers, Richard, 57-58, 205.

Class, Negro Middle
professions as representative of, 1.
composition of, 20, 199.
variation from other middle classes, 20, 200.

Color
role of in Negro life, 18.
relation to mobility, 30-31.
measurement of, 39.
role of mulattoes in Negro life, 104-108.
characteristics of respondents, 108-113.
of free Negroes and slaves, 199.

Davidson, Percy, 57-59, 70, 205.

Dentists (see Sample, Color, Occupations, and Family).

District of Columbia
Negro population of, 45.
occupational structure of, 45-46.
comparison with other large Negro communities, 45.
number of Negro medical specialists, 47.
variation from other urban areas in sample, 82.

DuBois, W. E. B., 207.

Duncan, Otis Dudley, 4, 5, 30.

Education
parents support of respondents' training, 94-99.
in relation to parental income, 99-101.
of respondents' parents, 101-102.

Edwards, Alba M., 57, 205.

Expected cases method, 51-52.

Family
motivation of southern respondents, 86-87.
income, 94-95.
influence on career selection, 121.
differences in structure of physician and dentist, 127-129.
role in support of physicians, 127, 132-133.
characteristics of respondents, 154-156.

Fitchett, E. Horace, 199.

Form, William, 146, 211.

Franklin, John Hope, 199.

Frazier, E. Franklin, 1-2, 19-20, 107, 199, 202, 206.

Free Negroes, 18, 20, 199.

Freedman, Ronald, 207.

Freeman Dental Society (see Professional Associations).

Freedmen's Hospital
role in training of medical specialists, 47.

Goldhamer, Herbert, 1, 106-107, 208.

Hall, Oswald, 132-133, 216.

Harris, Abram L., 5, 6, 200.

Hartshorn, Herbert H., 41, 134, 203, 209.

Hatt, Paul K., 29, 202.

Hawley, Amos H., 207.

Herskovits, Melville, 108, 110.

Houston, Charles, 137.

Howard University
role in training of Negro professionals, 46-47.

Income
in relation to support of education, 94-100.
and occupations entered by respondents, 99-101.
(see also Family).

Inheritance, occupational
relation to mobility, 67.
identical occupation, 67.
socio-economic status, 70-73.

Intelligence
measure of, 129.
differences between physicians and dentists in, 130.

Johnson, Charles S., 22, 23, 201.

Kluckhohn, Florence, 29, 202.

Lawyers
variation from other professions in motivating influences, 133-135.
career pattern, 150-154.
changing views toward Negro, 136-138, 210.

Lewis, Roy, 200.

Marital Status
of respondents, 42, 198.
(see also Family).

Maude, Angus, 200.

Medico-Chirurgical Society (see Professional Associations).

Migration
and formation of Negro communities, 25.
influence on background of respondents, 79.
and occupational mobility, 83.
relationship to education, 86-87.

Miller, D. C., 146, 211.

Mobility, occupational
in various social systems, 27-28, 202.
definition of vertical, 49; horizontal, 120, 164.
generational mobility, 62.
role of parents in mobility, 86.

Mobility (continued)
and economic status of parents, 99-101.

Moore, Wilbert, 199.

Mulattoes (see Color).

Myrdal, Gunnar, 19, 199.

National Opinion Research Center, 23, 60, 65.

Occupations
of respondents' fathers, 49-50, 52.
age and occupational background, 77-79.
variation in by regions, 79.
of paternal grandfathers, 62-67, 206.

Occupational Aspirations
of Negro youth, 21-23.
of respondents, 117-118.

Occupational Transmission (see Inheritance).

Parrish, C. H. , 39, 203.

Pierce, Joseph A. , 200.

Physicians (see Family, Occupations, Income, Sample, Color).

Professions
significance among Negroes, 1, 19-21.
relation to Negro middle class, 19-21.
increases among Negroes in, 23-26.
period in which decision made to enter, 131.

Professional Associations
use of rosters in selection of sample, 33.

in the District of Columbia, 47-48.

Regions
classification used in study, 39.
origin of respondents by, 44.
variation in mobility by, 79-81.
differences in support of education by, 98-99.
states included in each, 185.

Reid, Ira deA., 25.

Reiss, Albert J. , Jr. , 5.

Reuter, E. B. , 105-107, 208.

Rogoff, Natalie, 205.

Rose, Arnold, 107, 209.

Russell, John H. , 199.

Sample
criteria for selection, 31-32.
size, 35; estimates for teachers, 36.
comparisons with other professional populations, 41-42.
urban character of, 42-44.

Schedule, 36.
copy of, 175-183.

Social Differentiation (see Social Stratification).

Social Stratification
in early Negro life, 18-19.
as a process, 28.
in complex societies, 29-30.
and Negro migrations, 79.

Sibley, Elbridge, 208.

Sorokin, Pitirim, 70.

Statistical Tests, 40.

Teachers (see Sample, Occupation, Family).

Urban
    character of sample, 42-44.
    cities in Border region, 80-
        81, 207.
    urbanization and occupational
        inheritance, 71.
    influence on background of
        young respondents, 107.
    urbanization and color valua-
        tions, 107.

Walker, Harry J., 5, 210.

Washington Bar Association (see
    Professional Associations).

Washington, Forrester B., 201.

West Indies
    occupational origins of subjects
        from, 82.
    financing of educational costs,
        99.
    career pattern of subjects from,
        158-159, 169.

Williams, Robin M., Jr., 199.

Wolfe, Dael, 209.

Wirth, Louis, 1, 106-107, 208.

Woodson, Carter G., 23, 201.

Youth, Negro
    occupational choices of, 21-23.

Date Due